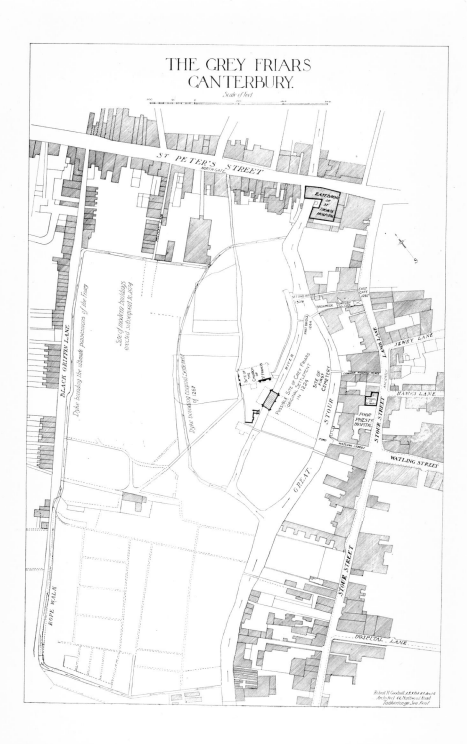

THE GREY FRIARS
CANTERBURY.

Scale of Feet

ST. PETER'S STREET

NORTH GATE

EAST DOOR OF ST. THOMAS HOSPITAL

Site of modern buildings erected subsequent to 1874

Dyke bounding the ultimate possessions of the Friary

Dyke bounding Original Settlement of 1267

BLACK GRIFFIN LANE

SECOND BRIDGE 1309

BROMMEDE

DUNGEY MILLING

EAST GATE 1267

FIRST BRIDGE 1264

RIVER STOUR

SITE OF THE CHAPEL OF ST FRANCIS

POSSIBLE SITE OF GREY FRIARS ORIGINAL SETTLEMENT IN 1224

SITE OF FIRST CEMETERY

STOUR

JEWRY LANE

LAND LANE

HAWES LANE

POOR PRIESTS HOSPITAL

ARCHES

STOUR STREET

WATLING STREET

FORD

WATLING STREET

GREAT

STOUR

STOUR STREET

ROPE WALK

HOSPITAL LANE

Robert H Goodsall, A.R.I.B.A & F.R.ml.S
Architect, 66 Northwood Road
Tankerton-on-Sea, Kent

SEAL OF GREY FRIARS, CANTERBURY
(A.D. 1294)

THE GREY FRIARS OF CANTERBURY

1224 TO 1538

A CONTRIBUTION TO THE 700TH ANNIVERSARY OF THEIR
ARRIVAL IN ENGLAND

BY

CHARLES COTTON, O.B.E., F.R.C.P.E.

HONORARY LIBRARIAN, CHRIST CHURCH CATHEDRAL, CANTERBURY

TOGETHER WITH A CHAPTER ON THE REMAINS OF THE FRIARY
AND ITS RESTORATION
BY

R. H. GOODSALL, A.R.I.B.A., A.I.Struct.E.

SECOND EDITION.

ILLUSTRATED BY MAPS, PLANS, VIEWS, ETC.

MANCHESTER: AT THE UNIVERSITY PRESS
LONDON, NEW YORK, ETC.: LONGMANS, GREEN & CO., LTD.
1926.

Published by the University of Manchester at
THE UNIVERSITY PRESS (H. M. McKechnie, M.A., Secretary),
23 Lime Grove, Oxford Road, MANCHESTER

LONGMANS, GREEN & CO., LTD.
London : 39 Paternoster Row, E.C. 4
New York : 55 Fifth Avenue
Toronto : 210 Victoria Street
Bombay : 53 Nicol Road
Calcutta : 6 Old Court House Street
Madras : 167 Mount Road

Printed in Great Britain by Lowe & Brydone (printers) Ltd., London. N.W.1.

PREFATORY NOTE.

This volume contains the text and illustrations of The Grey Friars of Canterbury, issued in 1924 by the British Society of Franciscan Studies, without the appendices. The references to appendices in the notes, are references to the original edition. Some information on the British Society of Franciscan Studies will be found on page 74.

11ᴰ· The Precincts,

Canterbury,

1926.

TABLE OF CONTENTS.

LIST OF ILLUSTRATIONS.

LIST OF ABBREVIATIONS OF TITLES OF BOOKS
AND MANUSCRIPTS REFERRED TO.

A. C. Wills.	Wills proved in the Court of the Archdeacon of Canterbury, at the District Probate Registry, Canterbury.
Anal. Franc.	Analecta Franciscana . . . edita a Patribus Collegii S. Bonaventurae (Quaracchi), 6 vols.
Ann. Monas.	Annales Monastici, ed. Luard, Rolls Ser., 5 vols.
Arch. Cant.	Archæologia Cantiana.
B.S.F.S.	British Society of Franciscan Studies.
Bull. Franc.	Bullarium Franciscanum, ed. Sbaralea, Eubel, etc., 1759-1908, 8 vols.
Brit. Mus. MSS.	Manuscripts in the British Museum (the Additional (Add.), Cotton, Lansdowne, and Royal Collections are referred to).
C. C. Wills.	Wills proved in the Consistory Court of Canterbury, at the District Probate Registry, Canterbury.
Cal. Close Rolls.	Calendar of Close Rolls prepared under the superintendence of the Deputy-Keeper of the Records.
Cal. Liberate Rolls.	Calendar of Liberate Rolls, Henry III, Vol. I, 1916.
Cal. Pap. L.	Calendar of Entries in the Papal Registers relating to Great Britain and Ireland : Papal Letters, Vols. I-X, 1893, etc.
Cal. Pat. Rolls.	Calendar of Patent Rolls.
Ch. Ch. Cant. MSS.	Manuscripts in the possession of the Dean and Chapter of Canterbury Cathedral.
Chron. Grey Fr.	Chronicle of the Grey Friars of London, ed. J. G. Nichols, Camd. Soc., 1852.
Close.	Close Rolls in the P.R.O.
Collect. Ang. Min.	Collectanea Anglo-Minoritica, or . . . Antiquities of the English Franciscans, by A. P[arkinson], 1726.
Collect. Fr. II.	Collectanea Franciscana, Vol. II, B.S.F.S., 1922.
Davenport, *Hist. Min.*	Historia Minor, by Christopher Davenport (Franciscus a S. Clara), 1658.
Dict. Nat. Biog.	Dictionary of National Biography.
Eccleston, ed. Little.	Tractatus Fratris Thomae vulgo dicti de Eccleston, ed. A. G. Little, Paris, 1909.
Excheq. Accts.	Exchequer Accounts in the P.R.O.

Gasquet, *Eng. Mon. Life.*	English Monastic Life, by F. A. Gasquet, 1905.
Gasquet, *Hen. VIII and Eng. Mon.*	Henry VIII and the English Monasteries, by F. A. Gasquet, 1888.
Gervas. Cant. Contin.	Historical Works of Gervase of Canterbury, ed. W. Stubbs, Rolls Ser., 1879, etc.
Grey Fr., Lond., Kingsford.	Grey Friars of London, by C. L. Kingsford, B.S.F.S., 1915.
Grey Fr., Oxf., Little.	Grey Friars in Oxford, by A. G. Little, Oxf. Hist. Soc., 1892.
Hasted, *Kent.*	History and Topographical Survey of Kent, by E. Hasted, 4 vols., 1778-98.
Hen. VIII, Froude.	Reign of Henry VIII, 3 vols., J. M. Dent.
Hist. MSS. Com. Rep.	Reports of the Royal Commission on Historical Manuscripts.
Inq. a.q.d.	Inquisitiones ad quod damnum, in P.R.O.
Kent Fines.	Lansdowne MSS., 267-269, in the Brit. Mus.
L. and P., Hen. VIII.	Letters and Papers . . . of the reign of Henry VIII, ed. J. S. Brewer and J. Gairdner.
Lambarde.	Perambulation of Kent, by W. Lambarde, 1826.
Lambeth MSS. Reg.	Registers of the Archbishops of Canterbury at Lambeth Palace.
Lanercost Chron.	Chronicon de Lanercost, ed. J. Stevenson, Bannatyne Club, 1839.
Liber Quotid. Cont. Gard.	Liber Quotidianus Contrarotulatoris Garderobae 28 Edw. I., 1787.
Liberate Rolls.	(Preserved in the Public Record Office.)
Lit. Cant.	Literae Cantuarienses, ed. J. B. Sheppard, Rolls Ser.
Little, *Studies.*	Studies in English Franciscan History, by A. G. Little, 1917.
Mon. Franc.	Monumenta Franciscana, Vol. I, ed. Brewer; Vol. II, ed. Howlett Rolls Ser., 1858, 1882.
Nicolas, *Test. Vet.*	Testamenta Vetusta, by N. H. Nicolas, 2 vols., 1826.
Pat.	Patent Rolls in the Public Record Office.
P.C.C.	Prerogative Court of Canterbury, Wills preserved at Somerset House.
P.R.O.	Public Record Office, London.
Rochester MSS., Reg.	Registers of the Bishops of Rochester.
Rolls Ser.	Chronicles and Memorials of Great Britain and Ireland . . . published . . . under the direction of the Master of the Rolls.
Reg. Epist. Peckham.	Registrum Epistolarum Fr. Joh. Peckham, ed. Trice Martin, Rolls Ser., 1882.
St. Franc., Fr. Cuthbert.	Life of St. Francis of Assisi, by Rev. Fr. Cuthbert, O.S.F.C., 1912.
Sever, *Eng. Fr.*	The English Franciscans under Henry III, by J. Sever, 1915.
Somner's *Cant.*	Antiquities of Canterbury, by W. Somner, 1640.
Spec. Perf.	Speculum Perfectionis, ed. P. Sabatier, 1898.
Supp. Monas.	Letters relating to the Suppression of the Monasteries, ed. by T. Wright, Camd. Soc., 1843.
Weever's *Fun. Mon.*	Ancient Funerall Monuments, by J. Weever, 1631.
Year Books, Edw. I.	Year Books of the reign of Edward I, ed. A. J. Howard, Rolls Ser., 1863, etc.

THE GREY FRIARS OF CANTERBURY.

CHAPTER I.

THE COMING OF THE FRIARS MINOR.

IT was just 627 years after the coming of St. Austin and his
companions to Canterbury, that another but smaller and more
insignificant party of missionaries arrived at the same place by
way of the Roman road known as the Watling Street. They
reached the City of St. Austin and St. Anselm a day or two after
they landed at Dover, on the Tuesday after the Feast of the
Nativity of the Blessed Virgin, which in the year 1224 fell upon
a Sunday. It was, therefore, the 10th day of September in the
8th year of the reign of King Henry III (1224) that they arrived
from France.[1] They were poor, so poor that they had not the
wherewithal to pay for their passage across the Channel, which
was defrayed by the charity of their friends, the Monks of
Fécamp in Normandy, which Monastery, at that time, had endow-
ments in England.

The party consisted of nine persons, four clerics of whom
only one was a priest, and five laymen; they were known as
Franciscans, Minorites, Friars Minor, Grey Friars or Barefoot
Friars. They were members of a recently established confra-
ternity of religious persons whose aim was to convert the masses
whom the Catholic Church at that time had failed to reach; they
took their name Franciscans from the name of their founder St.
Francis of Assisi who was still alive at this time, but who died
two years after their arrival. They were known as Minors or
Minorites as being the youngest and humblest of the religious
foundations, "less than the least," and Grey Friars from the
colour of their habits.

[1] *Eccleston*, ed. Little, p. 3.

This small band of men formed a very different spectacle from the dignified procession of the great Austin and his forty monks arrayed in black garments of archaic cut and fashion, preceded by the great Cross and the picture of our Saviour painted on a board.

The newcomers created no such sensation, it is doubtful if anyone turned out to watch them come in, for who would care to look at a few men dressed in coarse russet garments, patched with old sacking, and girded around their loins with a piece of old rope, the ends knotted to keep it from fraying? There was no processional Cross, no picture and no singing, unless perchance it was the *Bridal Song of the Virgin*, [1] sung by one of the party. They in sooth appeared a veritable gang of vagabonds, thieves or spies, as the writer of the *Chronicle of Lanercost* relates :—

> On their arrival in England they sought hospitality as mendicants at a nobleman's house near Dover, but they received it as strangers. For he locked them up in a strong chamber and bolted the entrance, that he might take counsel in the morning with his neighbours and examine who they were. All weary as they were the brethren betook themselves to rest until the day-break and then thinking to depart, they found the doors locked. They waited patiently, until later in the day they were brought forth before a crowd of on-lookers, and were asked who they were, and what might be their purpose in coming to this island. And when they had made known their purpose, one of the magistrates replied that they were spies and robbers. Whereupon one of them smilingly offered his cord and said, "if you take us for robbers, here is a halter ready to hang us with." Upon this, the judges returning to their senses, confessed that they who thus freely offered themselves to death could not have any evil purpose.

And they were allowed to depart.

They pursued their journey, passing along the Watling Street now known as the Old Dover Road, made and used by the Romans a thousand years previously. On reaching the last mile before arriving at the City of Canterbury they passed on their left the Hospital of St. Laurence founded for leprous monks of the Monastery of St. Austin by Abbot Hugh the second, scarcely a hundred years before in 1137. This hospital was built in the Norman style, with a Chapel attached, the entrance was from the road through a gate, the piers of which still remain; on the

---

[1] *Lanercost Chronicle*, p. 31. "Salve regina misericordiae" . . . "gloriosae virginis epithalameum." This hymn was usually sung after every office.

western-most is carved in stone a picture of the Martyrdom of St. Laurence, who is represented lying on his gridiron, with a man standing at his head, and another at his feet. This piece of carving was possibly the tympanum of the south or west doorway of the aforesaid chapel; and in the wall to the west of the piers may also be seen fragments of carved stone and one or more semi-circular headings of windows in the Norman style: these belonged to the same chapel, which was situate at the bottom of the garden of the house near by known as "St. Laurence Gate."

They, of course, could not see the Church which St. Austin passed on his way down St. Martin's Hill; that was obscured by the trees surrounding the Home Farm of the Abbey now called Barton Court; but could they have visited that church, a sight very different from that which St. Austin saw would have met their gaze. In his time St. Martin's Church, which had been restored for Queen Bertha's use, was a tiny building constructed after the Roman manner, and consisted of a small rectangular nave, terminating in a semi-circular eastern apse, dedicated to St Martin of Tours, at that time in the zenith of his popularity. At the time of the coming of the friars in 1224 it was much like what it is at the present day, except that the tower was wanting; this was not added till a century later.

There were one or two interesting sites which these friars would have passed on nearing the city, and first they would have noticed a "foot-path" emerging now by the side of the Old Forge House which crossing the main road passed up what is now called Ethelbert Road, at the top of which it strikes off across the fields in a south-easterly direction to Nackington, then called Natinton. Along this path which led directly from St. Gregory's Priory in Northgate (founded 1084) to the little Norman church of Nackington passed and re-passed the Augustinian canon who during the times when a secular priest had not been appointed as Vicar took the duty every Sunday and Holy day there during the four and a half centuries of the Priory's existence, in all weathers, wet and fine, wind and rain, frost and snow; as Nackington, like all other parish churches belonging to the Canons Regular, unlike those pertaining to the

Monastic Orders, was occasionally served by the canons themselves [1]

Nearer to the city, at the corner of Oaten Hill (the hill at the Oat Market) and the Watling Street, stood the Priory of St. Sepulchre, founded by St. Anselm *c.* 1100, for Benedictine nuns; always a poor convent, but as will be related hereafter, intimately concerned with the last phase in the history of the House of the Grey Friars of Canterbury. Across the main road here was St. Sepulchre's Bar, first noted as early as *c.* 1180 in a rental of Christ Church.[2] At Oaten Hill [3] was also a salt market, a place of execution for malefactors, and close by stood the market cross. In Somner's time (1640) it had "the cross still, but it was ill marketing at it." Here also, where "Nunnery Fields" now is, stood the city cattle market in ancient times.

The friars entered the city through the Roman Riding Gate and proceeded as far as the "Iron Cross," [4] where the four original streets of the Roman city met, and then passed up St. Margaret's Street and across the Middle Row at the west front of St. Andrew's Church which was then in the centre of the main street, continuing along the Mercerie and Palace Street to the Green Court Gate of the monastery, then known as the "Priory of the Holy Trinity." Here they were hospitably entertained for two days by the monks.

Our great local antiquary Somner, writing about 400 years after the coming of these friars and 100 years after the dissolution of their House, states that the date of their coming was the year 1224, and goes on to say—

How or where they were afterwards entertained with provision and accommodation of housing, I find not, until the year 1270.

It is curious that the tradition of the first settlement was entirely forgotten in 1640, and with all the research of modern times the *exact* spot still remains undetermined; as was also the site of the

---

[1] Gasquet, *Eng. Mon. Life*, p. 225. William, Prior of St. Gregory's Cant. was "Persona ecclesie S. Marie de Natyndon," June 1271. (Kent Fines, Hen. III, No. 1098.) William Crosse, Canon of St. Gregory's, adm., 4 March, 1462-3. Lambeth, Reg. Bourchier, fol. 86 ro.

[2] Ch. Ch. Cant., MSS. Reg. H., fol. 222 vo.   [3] Somner's *Cant.*, p. 149.

[4] Ch. Ch. Cant., MSS. Reg. H., fol. 225 vo.

4

original Priests' Hospice [1] (to be presently dealt with) until now. The fact that they had a lodging hereabouts is mentioned by Thomas of Eccleston, but it was only of a temporary nature lasting less than fifty years. After describing the sojourn for two days at the Priory of the Holy Trinity (Christ Church, where they were entertained by Prior John of Sittingbourne), he relates how four of them set off for London,

The other five went to the Priests' Hospice, where they remained till they found for themselves a dwelling. But very shortly after their arrival they were given a small chamber at the back of a school house where from day to day they remained almost continuously shut up during the day, but in the evening when the scholars had gone home they went into the school-room, and making a fire there sat around it.

It is said that at these evening conferences they would collect dregs of beer into a small pot, and after warming it would dip in it a cup and hand the cup round, each as his turn came speaking some word of edification. One who took part in this holy poverty has stated that

sometimes the beer was so muddy and sour that when the pot was to be placed on the fire they had to put in water to dilute it; and so they drank rejoicing.

The four who set off for London were known as Brothers Richard of Ingworth, a priest, Richard of Devon, an acolyte, Henry of Treviso, and a Friar named Melioratus. The remaining five were Brothers Agnellus of Pisa, who was a Deacon of about 30 years of age, and who had been appointed Provincial Minister or head of the new province of England; William of Ashby a novice; Laurence of Beauvais (a smith by trade); William of Florence; and James a novice. At the Priests' Hospice they came under the care of Alexander of Gloucester, the Master of the Hospice, who shortly after gave them a plot of ground and built them a Chapel sufficient for their needs, [2] evidently on the small island across the river which was the hospital garden as will be seen later. As the Order of Friars Minor had wedded Holy Poverty, and could possess nothing of

---

[1] The function of the Priest's Hospice may be recognized by its name; it was a Hostel for Priests and was probably attached to the Priory of the Holy Trinity (the Cathedral). Later it was under the patronage of St. Austin's Abbey.

[2] In the Cal. Liberate Rolls, I, p. 418, Alexander is mentioned as Warden of the Poor Priests of Canterbury, October 1239. See also Ch. Ch. Cant. MSS. C. 1152.

their own, the property was made over to the City, and held by the Corporation, who became, as it were, the Trustees of the House. This method of holding houses and lands was at the beginning the usual plan, and it is evident that the Citizens and Burgesses in most of the places where the Minors eventually settled (certainly in this country) were friendly to the Brethren and greatly assisted them in their work and ministrations amongst the poor.

As will be noticed later on, the number of benefactions the Canterbury Friars obtained from the citizens was large, and from their first settlement in the City they counted amongst their friends Simon Langton the Archdeacon of Canterbury, a son of Henry Langton and younger brother of the Archbishop; Sir Henry of Sandwich, the founder or re-founder of that beautifully situated Hospital of St. Bartholomew, outside the walls of Sandwich, and of its graceful Early English Chapel; and the " Noble Countess," as Thomas of Eccleston, the Chronicler of the Grey Friars calls her, " the Lady *Inclusa* de Hakington, who cared for the friars as a mother cares for her sons, wisely gaining for them the goodwill of princes and prelates by whom she was highly favoured." This lady was Lora or Loretta, daughter of William de Braose, Lord of Brecknock, and wife of Robert de Beaumont, called Fitzparnell, Earl of Leicester, who was Lord of the Manor of Haghe or Hawe in the Parish of Hackington near Canterbury. He died in 1204 without issue, and his widow becoming possessed of the Manor retired from the world and became a recluse (*Inclusa*) and devoted herself to the service of God at this place. She died probably about the year 1269,[1] and was buried in the Church of St. Stephen, Hackington, under a large stone lately to be seen in front of the steps leading to the Altar. It bore the figure of a woman with arms and other ornaments in brass, long since disappeared.

The fact that the five Canterbury Friars were lodged at first

---

[1] There is a record at St. Stephen's Church that this lady died about 1219. This is manifestly an error, as she was certainly alive on the arrival of the Grey Friars in 1224, and was a great benefactor to them as Eccleston states; she also pleaded for the Nuns of St. Sepulchre's Canterbury in 1256; Pat. 40 Hen. III, m. 2. (*Cal. Pat. Rolls*, p. 502); and as late as 29 April, 1265, is mentioned as still alive; see Bémont's *Simon de Montfort*, p. 101; Close Roll 49 Henry III, m. 6. d.

6

at the Priests' Hospice has caused some confusion amongst writers on the subject, who have apparently not identified this establishment with that of the "*Poor Priests' Hospital*," which still stands in Stour Street on its western side close to the river.

This really is the case: it was certainly in existence about 1218-20, and though it was further endowed by Archdeacon Simon Langton many years later, it was not founded by him, as has been usually stated. Some writers have suggested that the Hospital of St. John in Northgate, or the Hospital of St. Margaret is indicated as the asylum in which the Minors were entertained; but these are impossible, as the Hospital of St. John was strictly an asylum for the poor, infirm, lame or blind and aged men and women, and a Hospital of St. Margaret is not known even by name in Canterbury. This latter supposition may have arisen from the fact that the Poor Priests' Hospital was established in the Parish of St. Margaret, but it was dedicated to St. Mary. Its venerable remains, now sadly fallen from their former estate, are still to be seen in their entirety, part till recently being used as an emporium for second-hand furniture; but the southern portion, formerly the buttery and kitchen, the passage between the screens with minstrels' gallery over, and Refectory, is in the occupation of Messrs. Browne & Sons, the well-known Organ Builders.

As this hospital is contiguous to the site of the Friary shortly afterwards acquired by the Minors it may be well to say a few words concerning its foundation. On the north-west side of that part of Stour Street between Beer-Cart Lane (part of the Watling Street) and the High Street runs the eastern branch of the river Stour. This end of Stour Street was formerly called "Lamb Lane," and between the river and this lane about the year 1200, were [1] five tenements or houses with garden grounds attached in a block, bounded north by a narrow and short lane leading to the "common washing place" as described by Somner, and on the south by a similar lane connecting Beer-Cart Lane and the ford on the Stour, opposite to a small island, formed by a channel of the Stour dividing it from the larger island of Binnewith (which

[1] Ch. Ch. Cant. MSS. Reg. H. fol. 225 ro., and Cartæ Antiquæ, mentioned later. *See* also Somner's *Cant.* pp. 136-41.

itself lies between the two main branches of the Stour and upon which the western part of the city is built). The first of these, the house to the north, towards the High Street, but immediately south of the "common washing place" is recorded as being built of stone and was the house of Robert of Hotwell; this tenement was never part of the Poor Priests' Hospital; but its neighbour, the next to the south, the second of the block, situated opposite the opening of Hawks Lane is the northern portion of the site whereon the hospital was built. Up to the year 1218, it belonged to John Fitz-Godelef and Felicia his wife, who conveyed their house and land at "Othewelle" as it was called, near the bridge, south of the "common washing place" to Alexander of Glouces-ter. The instrument that records this transfer (Ch. Ch. Cant. C. 1181) is not dated, but from internal evidence can be fixed at about 1218.

The third house and tenement belonged to one Lambinus Flandrensis[1] (Lambin the Fleming or Lambyn Frese) from whom probably this part of the lane took its name. He was the son of Adam de Berghes, and possessed also a Mill there called Medmilne or Meadmilne, either because it stood midway between St. Mildred's Mill to the south, and the King's Mill to the north, or because it stood on the "meads" close by. Lambin also possessed some land in the island of Binnewith, probably in-cluding the small island opposite to his house, and being a pious man we read that he gave to Eastbridge or St. Thomas's Hos-pital (situated just below and built over the river, on land on the south side of High Street),

one seam (8 Bushels) of wheat from his mill and fourteen perches of land in the island of Binnewith, lying between the land or tenement of Samuel the Dyer towards the north, and the land of Godard the Miller towards the south on the river Stour.[2]

The fourth house to the south was that belonging to Godetha the widow of William Picot, which she granted to Lambyn Frese

[1] Godetha, relict of Wm. Picot, granted to Lambin Flandrensis, son of Adam de Berthes, and his heirs, all her claim to free bancumen (bench) in a messuage with appurtenances that Wm. Picot her husband had in the parish of St. Margaret, be-tween the stone house of the aforesaid Lambin north, and the messuage formerly of Richard the Plumber (which is held of Steven de Marsh), south, date c. 1218. Registry of Charters of the Poor Priests' Hospital, Canterbury. Brit. Mus. Add. MSS. 29, 437.
[2] Somner's Cant. p. 138.

about the year 1218; it was immediately north of the house of Richard the Plumber referred to in the same deed; the said house of Richard the Plumber being the fifth and completing the block, separated from the adjoining tenements in Stour Street proper on the same side, by the lane continuous with Beer-Cart Lane leading to the ford or waterlock.

To enter into a little further detail of the conversion of the above sites acquired by Alexander of Gloucester into the building for the purposes of a Hospice or Hospital, it will be seen from a personal survey of the remaining building that the southernmost tenement, that of Richard the Plumber, became the site of the buttery and kitchen. There is still to be seen on the side of the building next the river here, some very old half timber work (with dormer windows above), the joists and plates of which may date back to the time the Friars were entertained here.

Adjoining towards the north is the passage between the screens, with a fourteenth century doorway at either end; over the passage is a minstrels' gallery open into the Refectory to which access was obtained from an apartment above the buttery. There is a doorway in the centre of the passage towards the north entering immediately into the Refectory which is built on the site of the tenement of Godetha, relict of William Picot, which she conveyed to Lambyn Frese by charter quoted above, about the year 1218; Lambyn Frese conveyed it to Roger Frese (Ch. Ch. Cant. Reg. A. fol. 559^r), and Roger Frese conveyed it to Alexander of Gloucester (Ch. Ch. Cant. C. 1152). The charter which mentions this last transaction is of such interest to students investigating the site given to the Friars by Alexander of Gloucester at their first coming,—inasmuch as it states that Alexander himself was the founder of the hospital of which he was warden, and that the site of the Friars' earliest cemetery, and therefore of their first habitation of wattled cells, etc., was in the garden of the hospital,—that I have ventured to print it at length at the end of this chapter. All the above portions of the hospital are in the occupation of Messrs. Browne & Sons, Organ Builders.

Adjoining the Refectory, at its north end, and extending to

9

the land of Robert of Hotwell or Hottewelle, were two tenements, first that of Lambyn Frese mentioned above (Brit. Mus. Add. MSS. 29,437), and secondly that of John Fitz-Godelef and Felicia his wife (Ch. Ch. Cant. C. 1181), who conveyed their lands to Alexander of Gloucester about 1218-20, whereon was built the Entrance Hall and offices with dormitory above; and the chapel of St. Mary with the warden's lodging to the north, next to the land of Robert of Hottewelle. The Refectory opened by a door into the entrance hall and offices but is now walled up.

The east end of the chapel is flush with the street, but the Entrance Hall, Refectory and Buttery have a court in front facing the street. The whole building as now seen was rebuilt in stone in 1373 by Thomas Wyke, the then warden, with the exception of the half timber work at the extreme south-west corner already mentioned.

Simon Langton, Archdeacon of Canterbury, with the help of benefactions from the faithful became a benefactor and second founder of this asylum for Poor Priests, who, disabled by age or infirmity, were provided with a home and a Chapel, suitable for their declining years. The buildings are well worth a visit, the bell[1] in the small turret above the clock probably being the bell placed there in Thomas Wyke's time, which was tolled whenever the Abbot of St. Austin's Abbey passed that way, in acknowledgment of the jurisdiction of that Abbot and Convent over the institution.

Rather more than twenty years after the foundation of the hospital, at the request of Simon Langton, the same Abbot and Convent gave to the hospital in 1243, the Church of Stodmarsh; and in the year 1271, when Hugh Mortimer was Archdeacon, they also gave to it the Church of St. Margaret, Canterbury, in which parish the hospital stood.

It appears that the mill formerly belonging to Lambin was transferred to the hospital also, as in the year 1325, there was a suit before Robert of Malling, then Commissary of Canterbury, and he, after hearing the case, decided that this mill belonged to the Poor Priests' Hospital; it was nevertheless charged

[1] This seems to have disappeared during the war, as it is no longer in the bellcote.

with certain bushels of wheat to Eastbridge Hospital as before stated.

The small island immediately behind the hospital, and lying between it and that part of the large island called Binnewith belonged to this hospital, and served the Poor Priests as a garden. The large island, Binnewith, which name appears to be derived from the Saxon word "Binnan"[1] within, and withe, withy or willow from the Saxon word "withig," suggests the island within the willows; and later the name "with" was adopted as the surname of a family living on this island at the beginning of the thirteenth century. Somner (1640) mentions several members of this family as belonging to the island, such as John Binnewith, who in the beginning of the reign of Henry III was a benefactor to Harbledown Hospital, where may be seen his Charter and Seal, with "Sigill' Johannis de With" inscribed upon it: also Arnold Binnewith who was in 1221 and 1227 one of the Bailiffs of the City. It seems that towards the end of the thirteenth century the island was itself called Wytht, as in the Charter or Indenture[2] between the Prior and Convent of Christ Church, Canterbury and the Grey Friars, there is a tenement mentioned as formerly belonging to Berenger in Wytht; and it must not be forgotten that the whole island was as early as the reign of Kenulf, King of the Mercians, in 814, given to Wulfred, the Archbishop of Canterbury, as appears by his Charter.[3]

It is likely that almost up to the time of the Norman Conquest the island of Binnewith and its subsidiary islands between these two arms of the Stour were marsh lands whereon the willows grew, partly covered by water at high tides. The greater part of this land was brought within the walls of the city somewhere about the eleventh century, by the extension of the city westwards, and in the thirteenth century land on either side of the main street must have been fully built over, and the island drained. That particular portion westward of the Poor Priests' Hospital across the river, was very low-lying, and more or less

[1] Old English Binnan (prep. and adv.) = within, inside. For "with" cf. O.E. withig, withige, willow, withey. O.E. Binnen = M.E. Bine, Binne.
[2] Ch. Ch. Cant. MSS. C. 1031.
[3] Ch. Ch. Cant. Reg. P. fol. 17 vo; Kemble, Cod. Dipl. I, no. 205.

unhealthy in consequence. The history of this site and of its immediate neighbourhood has been dealt with more in detail, as it was here that the Friars Minor founded their first permanent English house.

POOR PRIESTS' HOSPITAL: RENTS PAID TO CHRIST CHURCH, A.D., 1418 (see p. 9).

Ch. Ch. Cant. MSS. C. 1152.

Memorandum quod cum anno Regni Regis Henrici quinti Anglie quinto mota et exorta fuisset quedam controuersia inter venerabiles et religiosos viros Dominum Johannem Priorem ecclesie x̄p̄i Cantuar' et eiusdem loci capitulum parte ex una et Dominum Willelmum Byngham ad tunc Magistrum siue custodem et Fratres suos hospitalis Pauperum Sacerdotum in ciuitate Cantuar' parte ex altera super quadam districtione capta in principali messuagio siue mansione eiusdem hospitalis per seruientes et ministros dictorum Prioris et capituli pro omnibus et singulis parcellis reddituum ad Thesaur' sancte ecclesie Christi annuatim de dicto hospitali soluendorum tam de mansione ipsius hospitalis quam de aliis diuersis terris et tenementis in diuersis locis dicte ciuitatis et surburbanis eiusdem diuersim iacentibus et dicto hospitali pertinentibus videlicet de mansione sua propria hoc (*sic*) ex (? est *but the parchment is defective*) aula cameris et capella sicut continetur in carta Rogeri frese facta Alexandro de Gloucestria fundatori dicti Hospitalis per annum Vs. Item pro Henrico Wode alias Deysye per annum ij s. iiij d. et pro Ricardo Bole per annum ix d. scilicet de duabus peciis terre contiguis iacentibus in gardino dicti Hospitalis inter sturam uersus East et South prope locum ubi olim fuerat cimiterium fratrum minorum cantuar'. Item pro Agnete Prowde per annum x d. de quadam terra que est iuxta domum predictorum Prioris et Capituli quam Johannes monde tenuit de eisdem. Item pro Forgabulo Guidonis textoris in parochia sancte Margarete per annum ij d. de quodam tenemento quod est inter tenementum Rogeri Barowner et tenementum Johannis Doul. Item pro Johanne de sancta Margareta per annum xiiij d. de quadam domo in Castelstrete inclusa. Item pro Andrea de Feretro per annum iij s. iiij d. ob. de quodam tenemento angulari in Castelstrete in angulo uenelle sancti Johannis. Item pro Johanne Duraunt per annum iij s. vij d. de grangia dicti hospitalis que est iuxta la dangon inter terram dictorum Prioris et capituli que uocatur merteghe uersus west et terram Johannis atte corner Chaundeler uersus east. Item pro Radulpho Turte per annum i d. ob. de quodam tenemento angulari super Fossat' inter regias Stratas uersus north et west in parochia beate Marie de Northgate tamen pro bono pacis et quiete partis utriusque de consilio et auisamento iuris peritorum una cum mediacione amicabili diuersorum amicorum partium predictarum dicta controuersia inter partes predictas anno supradicto taliter conquieuit uidelicet quod de cetero cum aliqua parcella reddituum predictorum in Thesaur' supradictam annuatim ut premittitur soluenda aretro fuerit in parte vel in toto aliquo anno futuro ad terminos solucionum eorundem reddituum limitatos et prefixos ex tunc

12

bene licebit prefatis Priori et Capitulo et successoribus suis per se vel ministros suos quos voluerint deputare parcellatim in principali messuagio siue mansione superius specificato pro redditu annuo quinque solidorum et in quacumque alia parcella superius specificata aretro existente distringere et districtiones captas abducere asportare effulgare et penes se retinere quousque de redditu ipsius parcelle sic districte plenarie et per omnia fuerit satisfactum set non in principali messuagio seu mansione dicti hospitalis pro totali et integro redditu omnium particulorum reddituum premissorum. In quorum omnium testimonium tam sigillum uenerabilis in x̄p̄o patris et domini domini Johannis Prioris ecclesie x̄p̄ī antedicte quam sigillum prefati domini Willelmi Byngham ad tunc magistri siue custodis Hospitalis Antedicti Hiis scriptis indentatis alternatim sunt appensa. Dat' anno supradicto.

The deed is sealed with what is perhaps the private seal of the Warden William Byngham. It is of red wax and bears a figure of the Agnus Dei, is $\frac{5}{8}$ inch × $\frac{6}{8}$ inch in measurement, and is attached by a slip of parchment to the Charter. There are two endorsements :—

(a) In a contemporary hand : " De redditu hospitalis pauperum sacerdotum in Cantuar' et suburbis."

(b) In a modern hand : "Indenture between the Prior and Convent of Christ Church, Canterbury, and William Byngham, Master or Keeper of the Brothers of the Hospital of Poor Priests in Canterbury, relative to several annual rents in the City of Canterbury and the suburbs thereof.

5th Hen. V. 1418."

CHAPTER II.

THE CANTERBURY SETTLEMENT.

I HAVE related above how shortly after the coming of the Friars Minor to Canterbury the Warden of the Priests' Hospice, Alexander of Gloucester, " made over to them a plot of ground and built them a chapel sufficiently becoming for the time," but that the actual site was a matter of surmise.   There is, however, a further reference written in the fifteenth century which occurs in the form of a memorandum in one of the MSS. in the possession of the Dean and Chapter of Canterbury, which throws some light on this point.   In Register O. fol. 407^v, appears this note : " In the year of our Lord's incarnation 1224 the Friars Minor arrived in England and were graciously received by King Henry, were lodged in Canterbury in Wyht, and in London on Cornhill." [1]

From this it would appear that on their arrival in England in 1224, the place in Canterbury where they were lodged was "wyht," i.e. on the Island of Binnewith, and as suggested in the last chapter, it was on that island which was the garden belonging to the Poor Priests' Hospital ; and therefore merely divided by one arm of the river from the later site given them by John Digge in 1267, to be related in this chapter.

The first buildings—wherever they were—must have been such simple dwellings as they put up in their other settlements, little cells of wattle, the walls filled in with dried grass or mud. Even the chapel built for them by their friend Alexander, was probably no better than the one they afterwards built at Cambridge, which was such a poor building, that Eccleston says "a carpenter made and set up the fifteen pairs of rafters" (which

---

[1] Printed in *Collect. Fr.* II, 9.   These notes from Register O. I have identified as the source from which the antiquary Leland obtained the information he gives in his *Collectanea*, which Weever and other writers have copied from him.

apparently formed the roof) in one day.[1]   They could not spend money on building at the first, for they had none; and we learn that so great was their zeal for poverty, that at Shrewsbury, where they were assisted in their building by King Henry III, and some wealthy burgesses, Friar William, the head of the English Province (Provincial Minister), at his visitation, ordered the stone walls of the dormitory which had already been built to be demolished and walls of mud to be erected instead.

The chapels of the friars were at first merely oratories to pray in, though they were allowed, the year they came to England, to celebrate Mass therein, provided a portable altar was used; this indulgence was granted to them by Pope Honorius III, 3 December, 1224.   The idea of an unconsecrated building with a portable altar was quite compatible with the spirit of absolute poverty they professed, as at any time such buildings could be turned to secular uses.   Later, certainly before 1250, the year that the Papal Bull *Cum tanquam veri*[2] established the use, they departed from this custom and their chapels or churches were considered conventual and were furnished with fixed altars, a proceeding which had given rise to some criticism as early as 1239 by Friar Hamo of Faversham, when he became Provincial Minister of England.[3]

The Friars Minor had wedded Holy Poverty, and according to the mind of St. Francis, poor building was as important as poor living, if they were to keep faithful to their Bride.   Eccleston relates the story of St. Francis appearing in a vision to Friar Robert of Slapton, at a place where some friars were temporarily lodged.   In the vision, the friars appeared to meet him, and to escort him to the *solarium* or upper chamber; then he looked about him a long time in silence.   At last the head of the house (the warden) said "Father, what are you thinking about?"   St. Francis answered "Look around at this house."   The warden looked and saw the whole house built of twigs, mud, and dung. St. Francis said, "Such ought to be the houses of the Friars Minor."

Nevertheless, the friars in England were assisted almost

---

[1] *Eccleston*, ed. Little, p. 28.
[3] *Eccleston*, ed. Little, 107-8.

[2] The date is 5 April, 1250.

universally by the populace, from the king on his throne to the beggar in his hovel, by gifts of land and materials for the foundation and building of their houses and churches, or by actual manual labour; the friars themselves sometimes co-operated in the work. At Oxford, John, late Abbot of Osney, who had joined the Order at Northampton in 1235, and Ralph of Maidstone, formerly Bishop of Hereford 1234-9, who had also taken the habit, are said to have assisted in the building of the Friary, carrying water and stones.[1]

The Canterbury friars continued to occupy the humble lodgings on their first site for nearly fifty years; but at length things were to change; the citizens had learnt to appreciate and value the friar, his work and influence, and especially his wonderful power of self-sacrifice, in all ages the one thing which is understood and recognized by the masses. Now the Grey Friar was to have a better and more fitting lodging more appropriate to an Order of men who had undoubtedly won the affection of the English laity by their life and conduct.

In 1267 a devout and worthy citizen, by name John Digge, an Alderman of Canterbury and a member of a prosperous and wealthy family then living in the city, who had been one of the Bailiffs[2] in 1258, and again in 1273, purchased some land on the other side of the river, immediately opposite to the Poor Priests' Hospital. This land consisting of several acres was in the east central part of the before described Island of Binnewith and south of the main street of the city, here called St. Peter's Street. It was where four of the city parishes adjoin and so lies partly within each, viz:—All Saints, St. Peter's, St. Margaret's and St. Mildred's; it was surrounded by a dyke and so formed an island. Alderman Digge made this over for the use of the Grey Friars, and shortly after transferred them hither. In the above quoted *Register O.* fol. 407ᵛ, may be found this note relating to the benefaction :—

"In the year of our Lord's Incarnation, 1267, John Digge

---

[1] *Anal. Franc.* III, 26 ; IV, 330.
[2] From A.D. 780 to 18 Henry III (1233) the city was governed by a Prefect, Portreeve, or Provost—in the latter year Henry III gave the citizens liberty to choose two Bailiffs yearly. It was not until 26 Henry VI (1448) that the Chief Magistrate became a Mayor.

bought the island in Canterbury called Binnewyght and the place of the gate upon Stour Street for the use of the Friars Minor, and transferred them thither at a convenient time."[1]

At a subsequent date other land was acquired, making up the total acreage to about 18 acres with orchards and gardens. The western boundary to this property appears to have been what is now called "Black Griffin Lane," formerly called "Mead Lane." There is some evidence as to the site and remains of the domestic and other buildings to be found in a map, published by William and Henry Doidge in 1752.[2] This map of Canterbury shows not only the mediæval building standing across the river as now, and the erections built up against it as depicted in many prints and early drawings on its north-west and south-east sides, but also a range of buildings to the south, apparently directly adjoining the site of the foundations recently uncovered by Major James. These are, I think, the remains of the original domestic building, and show a court in front towards the north, and two small courts on the south, each partly surrounded by the building itself. The map shows the dyke which enclosed the original plot of ground as given by John Digge, and also the considerable dyke surrounding the ground acquired later, on the north, on the west, and on the south, for the friars at the beginning did not surround their property with stone walls, but with ditches and palisades. The map shows "Griffin Lane" partly built upon and the lane then called Pocock's Lane, but at the present time St. Peter's Grove, the centre portion of which, 11 feet wide and 10 perches long, the Minors had appropriated in 1275, "to the serious injury of the City and County" though a few years after (in 1279) they obtained licence to enclose this road which then formed the western boundary of their ambit.[3] It is curious that the northern end of St. Peter's Grove for 70 feet in length is still 10 feet 3 inches to 11 feet in width; and that the lane from that point towards the south for 165 feet (10 perches) was only built upon about the year 1873, according to the Ordnance

---

[1] Printed in *Collect. Fr.* II, 9.
[2] St. Andrew's Churchwardens a/cs., *Arch. Cant.* Vol. XXXII, p. 183.
[3] P.R.O. Inq. a.q.d. file 5, No. 1; *Close Roll*, 9 Oct. 7 Edward I (1279); also see *Hundred Roll* (Rec. Com.), I, 203.

Survey; the rest of the present lane being garden ground at that time. Subsequently land was acquired westward as far as Black Griffin Lane, so called from an ancient tenement, probably an Inn of that name standing at the corner of the lane—the present public house being of much later date. This last acquisition was enclosed about 1392-3, as in the sacrist's accounts of Christ Church under that date occurs the following entry: " Item de iiij solidis de terra vocata Medland quia includitur per fratres minores." [1]

In 1336 [2] licence was given for alienation in mortmain by Master John de Romenale, Hugh le Woder, and William, parson of the Church of St. Mildred in Canterbury, to the Warden and Friars Minor of Canterbury, of a messuage and a garden 10 perches square, for the enlargement of their dwelling-place.

At the time of the suppression, [3] the property consisted of the church, bell tower, cemetery, the house and two messuages, two orchards, two gardens, 3 acres of land, 10 acres of meadow, and 4 acres of pasture in the parishes of St. Peter, St. Mildred, and St. Margaret, all held in chief of the Crown; and the boundaries of the property were :—on the north, the gardens of the houses in St. Peter's Street from St. Thomas's Hospital to Mead Lane (now called Black Griffin Lane); on the south, a dyke extending from the end of the Rope-walk to the Tannery in Stour Street; the river Stour on the east; and Mead Lane and its continuation under the name of the Rope-walk on the west; in all rather more than 18 acres, nearly all within a ring fence.

The entrance to the Friary from the main street, called the *Porta Borealis* was in St. Peter's Street in St. Peter's Parish; and a second entrance called *Porta Orientalis* was in Lamb Lane (Stour Street) in All Saints Parish. Previously the passage to a bridge before the friars took possession of the land, *c.* 1180, [4] was from the common washing place, between the tenement and garden of Robert de Hotwell to the south, and the stone house formerly belonging to Samuel the Dyer to the north. This latter

---

[1] Ch. Ch. Cant. MSS. Sacrist's Accounts, 1392-3 (reference kindly supplied by the Rev. C. E. Woodruff).

[2] *Cal. Pat. Rolls*, 10 Edward III, Vol. 1334-1338, p. 238.

[3] Hasted's *Kent*, Vol. IV, 448; *Arch. Cant.* XXXIV, 91.

[4] Ch. Ch. Cant. MSS. Reg. H. fol. 225 ro. and Somner's *Cant.* p. 139.

18

belonged to the Prior and Convent of Christ Church. It was released in 1242 by the Poor Priests' Hospital to Christ Church; but afterwards, in or before 1294, it with other tenements came to the Grey Friars, who in that year compounded with the Prior and Convent of Christ Church for the payment of 3s. in lieu of certain rents and tenements which belonged to Christ Church but were situate within the Grey Friars' precinct. These were the tenement (i.e. the Stone house) formerly held by Samuel the Dyer, which paid $7\frac{1}{4}$d., the two tenements formerly held by Berenger—one in With (12d.), the other in Ottemed (5d.): the tenement formerly held by Serona de Boctone (6d.); the rent of Wibert, formerly Prior of Christ Church (1151-67) for the tenement next to Ottewell (12d.); and the tenement held by Stephen, son of Lewin Samuel (1s. 6d.): a total of 5s. $0\frac{1}{4}$d. The Prior and Convent of Christ Church further remitted all the arrears then due, in consideration of the above-mentioned sum of 3s. which was to be paid every year into their Treasury, half at Easter and the other half at Michaelmas, by the proctors (or agents) of the friars.[1] The seal attached to this Deed is a very beautiful impression and in excellent condition. It is of brown wax, an elongated oval in shape, $1\frac{9}{16}$ inch long by 1 inch in breadth. It bears a representation of the martyrdom of St. Thomas Becket in the centre; the saint is kneeling before a vested altar with the hands upraised, and facing three of the knights, who with shields and raised swords are beating down the archbishop. There is a figure of Edward Grim, the Saxon clerk, from Cambridge, with the cross up-lifted standing at the far side of the altar. The apex of the seal is fitted with tabernacle work, and at the bottom is seen the tonsured head of a friar (St. Francis?) with his friar's hood falling over his shoulders. Around is this legend :—

S. FRATRVM MINORVM CANTVARIE.

On the coming of the friars, however, they required an entrance from the east to gain access to the site given them by

---

[1] Ch. Ch. Cant. MSS. C. 1031. Printed in *Collect Fr.* II, p. 1. With occasional default this sum of 3s. was paid up till the dissolution. Ch. Ch. Cant. MSS. Registers of Rents of the Estates belonging to the Priory, Case F. 2.

Alexander of Gloucester at the northern part of the island, forming the garden of the Poor Priests' Hospital.

There was in Lamb Lane, towards the north at the same distance from the common washing-place as the Watling Street is to the south of the common washing-place, another roadway or water-lock, leading to what was probably called Brokmede, which seems to have been in the possession of the friars at this time; for in the year 1264 they obtained "licence to build a bridge over the water of Stoure, between the site of their house, and their place called Brokmede, and to hold it to them and their successors for ever, so that boats (*navicule*) may pass under it without impediment, on testimony by the bailiffs and citizens of the City of Canterbury that this will not be a nuisance to the city." This was executed at Canterbury, no date is given, but it was about 20 August, 1264.[1] This bridge was probably of wood, and a similar bridge exists on this spot at the present time.

To the north of the above-mentioned roadway or water-lock was the piece of ground purchased by Alderman John Digge in 1267 as the "place of a gate" upon Stour Street for the use of the Minors, and it was here that the east gate was built, and subsequently a second bridge was thrown across the river from the north-west corner of this site to the island presented to them by John Digge.

This second bridge across the Stour was built of stone and brick and was not apparently made till the year 1309, as it is recorded in the *Calendar of Patent Rolls*, 3 Edw. II, that on 1 August, 1309

Licence (was given) for the alienation in mortmain, after inquisition *ad quod damnum*, by John de Burne, to the Warden and Friars Minor of Canterbury, of a roadway from the highway to the water of the Sture. Licence also for them to build a bridge across the Sture extending from the above roadway to their dwelling house for the benefit of persons wishing to attend service in their Church; the bridge to be so built as to allow a clear passage for boats underneath it.

From this it also looks as if the stone bridge did not have more than two arches originally, and that the passage was effected by one arch being of greater span than the other to allow the passing

[1] *Cal. of Pat. Rolls*, Hen. III, 1258-66, p. 342.

Grey Friars, Canterbury. Friars Bridge, 14th Century

GREY FRIARS, CANTERBURY, BEFORE 1844

From a drawing by F. W. Fairholt, F.S.A.

Photograph by J. G. Charlton

of boats—if this be so, it was the very wide eastern arch which was removed in 1589, when the then owner William Lovelace covenanted with the Mayor and Commonalty to take down the stone bridge which led from Lamb Lane to the Grey Friars, as the westernmost of the two arches still remaining is clearly of mediæval construction.

The north gate stood in that part of the main street here called St. Peter's Street, almost opposite the mediæval St. Peter's Gate of the Black Friars, which was at the entry of the street now called "The Friars."[1] This north gate led down a lane, which was 25 feet wide, directly to the west door of the Friars Church and Churchyard. Its site is now occupied by a shop erected in the early seventeenth century, with a passage of 4 feet 6 inches on its western side, which still leads down to the ruined west door of the Church. I have not come across any view of this gate, except one in the bird's eye view of the Black Friars estate drawn in 1595 by Thomas Langdon where it is shown as an embattled gateway with a depressed arched opening and window or niche on either side, exactly like the gate of the Black Friars opposite. Drawings of this latter have been preserved; it was erected not long before 30 Edward III (1356), and consisted of a high wall with a kind of penthouse roof of tiles with a fourteenth century archway beneath. A panelled and decorated string course went across at the level of the spring of the arch on either side; above the string course were decorated niches one above the other with apparently good fourteenth-century tabernacle work; the gateway had stone quoins, and was faced with black flints. The copper plate of this gate was drawn by T. Six and published in 1792. It was taken down in 1788.

The western boundary of the friars was Black Griffin Lane; in mediæval times, to be identified with Mead Lane,[2] and at an earlier date it was called Crinemelne Lane. At that time there

[1] There is a very faded document in the Cathedral Library (C. 1225) measuring 11 inches by 8⅝ inches, dated the 28th year of Edward I (1300), being a copy of an instrument relative to the Rents of the Grey Friars of Canterbury. It is between the Warden and Convent, and one William of Dover, citizen of Canterbury; by it the said William is enfeoffed by Thomas son of John Digge, of the Parish of All Saints, Canterbury, and undertakes to pay a certain rent for the house he is allowed to build and also covenants not to make a window or opening looking out on to the road or way by which the Friary is entered from the north gate.
[2] See map of the City in Somner's *Cant.*

were certainly tenements, shops and gardens in Mead Lane, as well as property belonging to the Nuns of St. Sepulchre's Priory, and other persons, as may be seen from the demise[1] executed in 1397, by Thomas Ickham of Canterbury, to John Ropere of Westgate, and Thomas Smyth of Canterbury of two shops with gardens, etc., situated in Mead Lane in the Parish of St. Peter.

Though the Friars Minor were not an enclosed and secluded Order, like some of the monastic Orders, the Canterbury Friary certainly had a surrounding wall, so far as the Church, its yard, and the domestic buildings were concerned, but it is doubtful how much of the present wall is of mediæval date. That the whole Ambit was enclosed later is probable, as a reference to the Map of Canterbury, published by Somner in 1640, shows enclosing palisades or walls, notwithstanding the story which Eccleston relates, that when a certain friar jokingly said that he would accuse Friar William, the Provincial Minister, to the Minister-General for not enclosing the London Friary, Friar William retorted, "And I will tell the Minister-General that I did not become a Friar for the purpose of building walls." But this of course refers to an earlier period.

There is amongst the Archives of the City a volume entitled "A collection of sundry extracts, instruments, letters and papers, taken principally from the records in the Chamber of Canterbury respecting the Four Houses of Friars within the City of Canterbury." They were collected by Alderman Bunce in and before 1802 and contain a large amount of matter dealing with the

---

[1] Ch. Ch. Cant. MSS. C. 1042ᵇ. Sciant presentes et futuri quod ego Thomas Ickham de Cantuaria demisi concessi et hac presenti cart [a mea confirmaui] Johanni Ropere de Westgate et Thome Smyth de Cantuaria duas schopas cum gardin' annex' et pertin' suis in Parochia Sancti Petri in Cantuaria in Medlane scituat' inter [*the word here is undecipherable*] in Medlane uersus east et tent' Johannis Haute uersus west et gardin' Priorisse et conuentus mon' sancti Sepulchri Cantuar' uersus south et tent' dict' Priorisse et conuentus et tent' Johanne Marchal uersus north habendum et tenendum predictas duas schopas cum gardin' et pertin' suis prefatis Johanni Ropere et Thome Smyth heredibus et assignatis suis de Capitalibus dominis Feodi illius per servicia eis inde debita ac iure consueta imperpetuum. In cuius rei testimonium huic presenti carte mea sigillum meum apposui. Dat' cantuarie festo sancte Katerine uirginis et martyris anno regni Ricardi secundi Angl' uicesimo [Hiis testibus] Stephano Sellynge Johanne Harnhell Balliuis Cantuar' Johanne Cherche senʳ. Ricardo Godefrey [Thome] Poldre Willelmo. . . . Meed Johanne Chaundeler Ricardo Maydestone Roberto Boklond et aliis. (Thomas Ickham was Jurat of Canterbury, 1397-9 and again in 1401; Stephen Sellynge and John Harnell were Bailiffs of Canterbury, 1397-8; Richard Maydestone was " scrutator molendi " in 1396-1404. Canterbury City Archives, Book of Accounts, 1393-1445.)

Black, Grey, Austin Friars, and also those of the Sack; it is un-
fortunate that the papers dealing with the Franciscans are but
few in number, and refer principally to the alienation of the
House and land at the Dissolution. There is one document of
interest which might be introduced here, and that is a rough plan
or map of the City showing the position of the Three Houses of
Friars within the walls. The map is endorsed "This sketch
was made at the time of the City's dispute with Mrs. Margaret
Hovenden about the 'way' through the Black Friars and was
used with the pleadings in the suit 1595." Our interest lies in
the direction of the "ways" through the Grey Friars Ambit
from either gate, north and east. That through the north gate
passed down to the west door of the church, and about half-way
down at a point opposite the east gate, it turned directly at right
angles to the east and joined the way from that gate after it had
crossed the river. The north gate remained till after 30 September, 1595, as it is shown in the drawing of the Blackfriars
of that date, soon after which it was pulled down, and the existing house built on the site.

Of the east gate no drawing has come down to us; the house
now No. 6 Stour Street, erected also in the seventeenth century,
stands on its site; a passage through and on its southern side
leads directly to the wooden bridge, and a narrow one to the
north to the stone bridge. Within and between these two gates
the Friars Minor, about the year 1267, built their permanent
home (a very different one to that which had housed them for
the previous forty years), comprising, if the house was planned
after the model of their houses elsewhere, a Friary Church,
Cloister, Refectory or Frater, Dortor,[1] Chapter House, Studies,
Library and Infirmary.

Alas! only one building above ground has remained at
Canterbury. This is the Early English building under which
the river Stour passes, consisting originally of one floor only
above the ground floor—though after the Dissolution it was
altered many times by being turned into a private house, a gaol,

---

[1] William Byllynton of the Parish of All Saints, Canterbury, who died 21
November, 1444, in his will proved 13 January, 1444-5, "lego fabrice de le Dortour
Fratrum minorum Cantuar. decem libras." Lambeth MSS. Reg. Stafford, 125b.

and back again into a private house. In modern times it has often been drawn, painted and photographed, being one of the most picturesque buildings in the City and in a most beautiful and romantic setting. In 1844 it was drawn by F. W. Fairholt for the *Archæological Album* issued in commemoration of the visit of the British Archæological Association to Canterbury. This drawing shows the original building with its beautiful Early English arches spanning the river, its lancet window above, and attached on both sides are pre-Reformation portions of the convent, including the outside staircase as at the Lincoln House; with some ruined walls, a doorway, etc., about the court. Fortunately parts of the west doorway and wall of the church, its foundations, and some few foundations of the domestic buildings to the south have been recently discovered, and it is hoped that when the site has been more fully excavated a plan of the house will be available. Those fragments which remain are beautiful examples of Middle and late Early English architecture.

The existing portions of the church show that it was built of rough field flints with stone dressings; the west doorway and the windows had attached shafts to the jambs on either side with moulded bases and caps of plain Early English design, without foliage. In its plan the church was long and narrow, characteristic of the friars' churches which were intended to provide a suitable nave for preaching in. From careful measurements taken, its extreme length from the east chancel wall to the west nave wall was 77 feet, and its extreme width was 27 feet—the width of the south wall of the church was 2 feet 6 inches. Compared with the mediæval nave of the Parish Church of St. George, which is fairly typical of the city churches, it was only 8 inches less in length (including the space under the tower at the west end at St. George's), and was actually 9 feet wider. From these measurements one is justified in believing that the Friars' Church here had a " walking-place " between the choir and the nave, called also " the belfry," which was a unique feature in the Minors' churches in this country; upon it was built the Bell-tower, mentioned in several deeds, surmounted by a light steeple as in their churches at London,[1] Lynn, and Richmond. In Braun

[1] *Grey Fr. Lond.*, Kingsford, p. 41.

and Hogenberg's *Civitates Orbis Terrarum*, published at Cologne in 1572, is a plan, map, or bird's-eye view of the city, drawn thirty-two years after the general dissolution of the religious houses, when much destruction had doubtless already taken place. Here the Friars' Church is depicted as a long narrow church with transepts and a tower and steeple at what is evidently meant to be its west end, though the church is placed on the map north and south. This plan is of considerable archæological interest, being the earliest known of the City; it is, however, manifestly incorrect in many particulars. There is another map drawn by William Smith in 1588; it is a reduced and rather inaccurate copy of Braun's view, and throws no further light on the matter in question.

The peculiar arrangement of the "walking place" between the choir and the nave, with a door at either end of it north and south, allowed of a choir for the friars of considerable privacy; from a statement made by Anthony Parkinson, the high altar was dedicated to St. Francis.[1] The nave screen separating the east end of the nave from the "walking-place," would have an entrance in its centre surmounted by the rood,[2] and this screen would serve as a reredos for an altar placed towards the north, dedicated to St. Clement,[3] and one on the south dedicated to Our Lady.[4] In the London House the Guild of Bakers used the altar of St. Clement, but though there was a Fraternity of Bakers in Canterbury I cannot find that they used this altar here. A Guild of Corpus Christi was connected with the church.[5]

In the will of Bishop Richard Martyn,[6] mention is made of the Chapel of the Holy Saviour within the Grey Friars Church, and of a "Chapel Chamber" in which the bishop's great bed stood. This chapel, apparently, was built out on the south side of the nave just to the west of the nave screen; the excavations on this part of the site show that a break occurs at a distance of 27 feet from the east end of the south wall of the church, and

[1] *Collect. Ang. Min.* Pt. II, p. 12.
[2] *See* will of Margaret Cherche, in Appendix.
[3] *See* will of John Forde, in Appendix.
[4] *See* will of Alexander Elyothe, in Appendix.
[5] Will of Agnes Bochard, 1492.
[6] *See* his will, in Appendix.

there are considerable remains of buttressing now uncovered. It is possible that the "Chapel Chamber" was built above this chapel, like the room over the chapel now used as a vestry on the south side of the Parish Church at Rye.

Bishop Richard Martyn left to the friars, amongst other things, his crismatory of silver and gilt in a case, a standing cup of silver, and ten books for their library ; as well as altar cloths, a vestment, chasuble, two candlesticks of latten, and two cruets belonging to the chapel.

Many of the laity left directions to be buried in this church, and had memorials erected over their tombs, as Thomas Barton,[1] Gent., of Northgate, who died in 1476 : "A little square stone of marble be set in the wall over the place where I shall be buried," upon which was to be graven the image of Our Lady and the four evangelists, and the figures of his father and mother, of himself and his wife, his children, and an inscription to be made so that the people might remember his soul. Hamo Bele [2] of Elham, in 1492, desired to be buried in the middle of the nave of the church and directed that a tomb 3 feet high should be set up over him and Elizabeth his wife. Doubtless also those knights and ladies mentioned amongst the benefactors of the House in Chapter IV, had suitable tombs erected over their remains. With regard to the burial of Sir William de Baliol, Knight, there is an instrument amongst the muniments of the Dean and Chapter dated 8 June, 1312, and endorsed [3] "Covenant between Henry,[4] Warden, and the Convent of the Friars Minor of Canterbury, and the Prior and Chapter of Christ Church, Canterbury, etc. etc.," which concerns the burial of Sir William de Baliol in a fit and proper place within the Friars' Ambit.

The churchyard was on the north side of the church, and must have been of considerable extent to judge from the number of persons desiring to be buried therein.

The church was built subsequently to 1267 ; it was not con-secrated till 1325, when Archbishop Walter Reynolds himself performed the act of consecration.[5]

[1] *See* his will, in the Appendix.   [2] *Ibid.*
[3] Ch. Ch. Cant. MSS. F. 152. The text is printed by me in *Collect. Fr. II.*
[4] This was Henry of Chibalton (Chilbolton, Co. Hants).
[5] Lambeth MSS. Reg., Reynolds, fol. 186v.

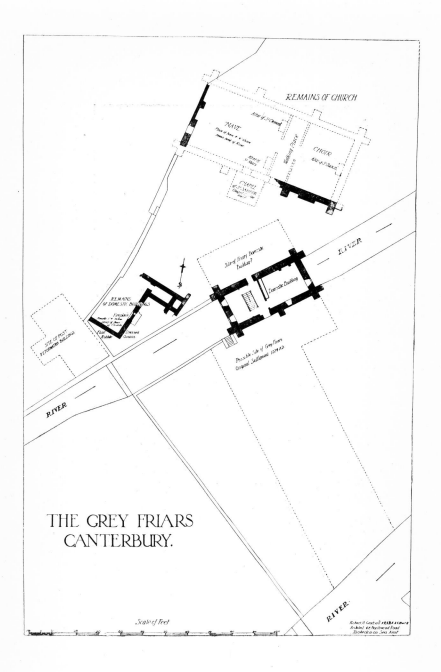

REMAINS OF CHURCH

"NAVE"

Altar of St Clement

Burying Place

CHOIR

Altar of St Mary

CHAPEL OF ST SAVIOUR

Site of Friary Domestic Building?

Domestic Building

REMAINS OF DOMESTIC BUILDINGS

SITE OF POST REFORMATION BUILDINGS

Possible Site of Grey Friars Original Settlement 1224 AD

RIVER

RIVER

RIVER

THE GREY FRIARS
CANTERBURY.

Scale of Feet

Robert H Goodsall FRIBA FSA
Architect 66 Northwood Road
Tankerton on Sea Kent

GREY FRIARS, CANTERBURY, 1923

Photograph by Youngman & Son

Besides the beautiful building over the river and the few foundations of the church and domestic buildings lately uncovered, there are remains of stone doorways (one, in a complete condition, of the fifteenth century), carved stones and ashlar built into post Reformation walls, etc., etc. The domestic buildings extended westwards and southwards into adjoining property, no part of which has as yet been excavated; the foundations here should prove of great local as well as of general interest, in determining the ground plan of the Friary and its arrangement, when uncovered. Nor should the visitor neglect to examine the early fourteenth century Friars' bridge across the Stour near where was the East Gate.

CHAPTER III.

WE have followed the history of the Canterbury Friars down to the time when their house was permanently established, and the new church and churchyard consecrated. It will now be necessary to give a short account of their work and the way their Order was organized for the due performance of it. The third and last note concerning these friars in the above quoted *Register O.* in the Cathedral Library is as follows on fol. 407[v] :—

In the year of our Lord's Incarnation 1226 Blessed Father Francis, bearing the stigmata of Jesus Christ, left this present state of exile and joined the Heavenly throng ; and so the Brothers Minor came to England, two years before the death of Blessed Francis.[1]

By the beginning of the thirteenth century the Church had done little to adjust itself to the intellectual and economic changes which were affecting the thoughts and lives of men. This was the work of the two great Mendicant Orders, the Dominicans and Franciscans.

Some of the friars who came to England in 1224 were in close personal touch with St. Francis and were filled with his spirit. Thus the lay brother, Laurence of Beauvais, who worked "*in opere mechanico,*" according to the Rule, recalls the life of primitive Franciscanism. "He returned later to St. Francis, and was held worthy to see him often and to be consoled by his conversation ; the holy father at last gave him his tunic, and sent him back to England gladdened with a most sweet blessing." [2]

The friars were missionaries, who preached more by example

---

[1] Printed in *Collect. Fr.* II, p. 9.   [2] *Eccleston*, ed. Little, p. 7.

than by words; and it was St. Francis, who, as Mr. J. S. Brewer says in the *Monumenta Franciscana,*

first stripped Christianity of the regal robe in which Popes and Prelates had invested it, and then preached it as the Gospel of the poor and the oppressed; he caught the poorest in their poverty; the subtle in their subtlety; sending among them preachers as ill-clad and as ill-fed, but as deep thinkers in all respects as themselves. His followers are to visit the towns two and two; in just so much clothing as the commonest mendicant could purchase. They are to sleep at nights under arches, or in the porches of desolate or deserted churches, among idiots, lepers, and outcasts; to beg their bread from door to door.

They were to settle in the suburbs amongst the dregs of the population. In Canterbury we find them in the low, swampy and undrained isle of Binnewith, through which the river flowed, and into which refuse and garbage, such drains as existed and other filth found their way; to say nothing of the cold mists and raw fogs blowing across the marshes in winter.

St. Francis in a conversation with a benefactor [1] described the method that his brethren should adopt when a piece of land was given to them to build a Friary upon. Having obtained the blessing of the bishop of the diocese, they were to make a deep ditch [2] round the land with a good fence instead of a wall as an emblem of their poverty; their cottages were to be of mud and wood, with some few cells for the friars to pray and labour in for the eschewing of idleness. They were to have small churches and not large ones. These poor houses, cells, and churches would be their best sermons. Rigid poverty continued to be the rule in England till the dissolution, as may be seen from an examination of the King's Visitors' Reports in the 30th year of Henry VIII.

The "*Speculum Perfectionis*" describes the Minors' devotion to the nursing of lepers [3] and attendance on the sick. It is difficult in these days to realize the condition of the leper in the last stages of his terrible complaint, when sweet herbs soaked in

[1] *Spec. Perf.*, ed. Sabatier, Cap. 10.

[2] In the Ordnance Survey Map of the City of Canterbury, 1873, can be seen the ditch filled with water around the original site of the Grey Friars, i.e. enclosing the plot of ground granted them by Alderman John Digge in 1267.

[3] Leprosy existed in England as an endemic disease up to the fifteenth century. After that date no new leper hospitals were built. The last one of any note was founded at Highgate in 1472. Robert Liveing on "Leprosy" in Quain's *Dict. of Med.*, Vol. I, p. 1100, 1895.

warm water occupied the place of carbolic acid or Lysol as a disinfectant and deodorizer. The Minors knew that their mission would bring them amongst the poorest of the poor, the cast out of the outcast and the sick so loathsome that their disease was a crime, dealt with practically by imprisonment; yet their recruits in these early times were drawn especially from the educated classes and those of gentle birth; these men were able to overcome the natural repulsion of refined natures, to give up all the material things which make life tolerable, and to wed "Holy Poverty" for the Kingdom of Heaven's sake.

But the Franciscan fraternity had already gone through various phases before the friars came to England. The association of brothers had become an Order with a definite noviciate and a Rule authorized by the Pope. The friars, who at first had continued to work at their ordinary employments, had begun to live a community life in settled houses. The care of lepers had almost ceased to be any special concern of the Order, and manual labour was giving place to preaching. The lay element was, however, still strong and was not definitely subordinated to the clerical till 1240.

The great increase in the Order had necessitated changes in its organization, and a strengthening of the bonds of discipline and authority. The great annual assemblies of all the brethren had been superseded by small triennial conferences of the principal officers. These conferences or General Chapters were subsequently reinforced by regularly elected representatives of the friars; but no provision for them is made in the Rule of 1223: the constitutional change seems to have been made in 1240— at a time (it may be noted) when a native of Kent, Hamo of Faversham, was Minister-General.[1]

At this time (c. 1240) the Order was organized as follows :— [2] At the head was the Minister-General assisted by the Chapter-General which met every three years and had power to depose and elect the Minister-General. The Chapter-General contained the Provincial Ministers, and elected representatives of each of the

[1] Cf. *Anal. Franc.* III, 246 ; *Eccleston*, ed. Little, pp. 86-9.
[2] On the constitution of the Order, see Holzapfel, *Handbuch der Geschichte des Franziskanerordens* (1909), pp. 171-205.

provinces. There were thirty-two (eventually thirty-four) provinces, at the head of each of which stood an elected Provincial Minister, with a Provincial Chapter meeting every year and consisting partly of officers (such as custodians and wardens), partly of elected representatives of the houses. In each province the houses were formed into groups called Custodies with a Custodian over them, and the head of each House was called Guardian or Warden. England was divided into the seven custodies of London, Oxford, Bristol, Cambridge, Worcester, York, and Newcastle. Canterbury was one of the eight houses[1] which formed the custody of London in the Province of England.

Within thirty-two years of their coming (1256-7) the friars in England numbered 1242, and the friaries forty-nine. After this time the rapid increase of houses was stayed, though the average number of inmates in each was somewhat larger. In the next fifty years only nine more houses were added, and the number of friars about A.D. 1300 has been calculated at a little less than 2000.[2]

We have the means of estimating accurately the number of Friars Minor at Canterbury during some fifty years (1289-1336). It was the custom of the kings when they visited a town to give a pittance or allowance for food to the various houses of friars, generally at the rate of 4d. a day to each friar. Thus in August 1289, Edward I gave 60s. to the Friars Minor and 50s. to the Friars Preachers of Canterbury for three days. This would seem to imply 60 Friars Minor and 50 Friars Preachers; but as these numbers are far in excess of any subsequent numbers, we must assume either that double rations were supplied on this occasion or (more probably) that for some reason or other, there was a great and temporary influx of friars.[3] In June, 1297, the King gave to the Friars Minor 39s. by the hand of Friar Durand of Cornwall, and 31s. to the Friars Preachers, again for three days.[4] The numbers were 39 and 31 respectively. From similar records it appears

---

[1] Namely London, Salisbury, Canterbury, Winchelsea, Southampton, Lewes, Winchester, Chichester.

[2] Little, *Studies*, 68-72.

[3] P.R.O. Exch. Accts., 352 (18). It may be noted that the Friars of the Sack on this occasion received 3s.

[4] Brit. Mus. Add. MSS. 7965, f. 8v. (Friars of the Sack again 3s.).

that the Friars Minor numbered 34 in 1299, 30 in 1300,[1] 35 in 1320, and 37 in 1336.[2]

The Franciscan friary was the largest of the three in Canterbury. It was not among the largest Franciscan houses in England, but was in numbers rather above the average. These royal alms ceased at the beginning of the French war, and so we get no information from this source as to the effects of the Black Death in the friaries.

The Canterbury House does not seem to have played so important a part in the life of the Province as we should have expected from its situation in the ecclesiastical capital of England. No evidence has yet come to light of any Provincial Chapter having been held here (with one doubtful exception)[3] until 1532. Nor does the House appear to have produced any famous sons. Friar Hamo of Faversham, provincial and then general minister (1239-44), probably visited the convent, but he had entered the Order at Paris in 1223. John Pecham derived his name not from Peckham in Kent, but from Patcham in Sussex, and probably had no connexion with Canterbury till he became Archbishop. A Friar Roger of Canterbury was Warden of London in 1257, and another London warden, John Bruyll (1398), seems to have been a Canterbury friar. But the lists of theological lectors at Oxford and Cambridge contain no names which imply a Canterbury origin.

The House was, however, early recognized as a place of study. Albert of Pisa, Provincial Minister in 1236, appointed Henry of Coventry as lecturer here.[4] And though the House was never a *studium generale* in the Order nor even apparently a school for the custody of London, the remains of its library tend to show that its inmates did not neglect learning. It will be remembered that the English Province supplied the Franciscan Order with its most original thinkers—Roger Bacon, Duns Scotus, William of

[1] P.R.O. Exch. Accts. 355 (18). *Liber Quotid. Contrarot. Gard.* 28 Edw. I, p. 30.
[2] Brit. Mus. Add. 17362, f. 4; Cotton Nero, C. VIII, f. 205v.
[3] A chapter was held on 8 September, 1316, at " Cant' " (Wardrobe Acct., 10 Edw. II, p. 19, in the possession of the Society of Antiquaries); this may be Canterbury or Cambridge. On the chapter in 1532, see p. 52 below. Sever, *Engl. Fr.,* p. 117, places a chapter at Canterbury in 1240. It was really held at Cambridge : *Cal. Close Rolls,* Hen. III, p. 208.
[4] *Eccleston,* ed. Little, p. 62.

32

Occham—and a long line of learned and distinguished scholars, such as Adam Marsh, John of Wales, Thomas Dockyng, Thomas Bungay, Archbishop Pecham, Richard Middleton, to name only a few.

Among the books formerly in the library of the Grey Friars of Canterbury [1] was a *New Testament* with gloss., now in the British Museum,[2] given them by Friar Ralph of Maidstone, who was Bishop of Hereford 1234-9. In 1253 Richard Wych (St. Richard), Bishop of Chichester, bequeathed them a copy of the *Book of Isaiah* with gloss.[3] There are five other volumes now in the British Museum which belonged to this library, namely :—

A series of thirteenth-century Biblical manuscripts in Latin : (1) *Genesis* and *Exodus*, with gloss. ;[4] (2) *Isaiah, Jeremiah,* and *Daniel,* with gloss., and lists of the kings of Persia, Egypt, and Syria, given by Master Adam of Richmond, and containing the press-marks ".B. " and "C.4. ";[5] (3) the *Gospels of St. Mark and St. Matthew,* with very full gloss., and the press-mark " D.23 ";[6] (4) the *Epistles of St. Paul,* with commentary of Peter Lombard, the gift of Friar Henry of Rye.[7] Another volume of the thirteenth century containing Geoffrey of Monmouth's *Historia Britonum,* the *Historia Hierosolimitana* of James of Vitry, *Gesta Alexandri* and *Historia Romanorum,* and the *Chronicle* of Martin of Troppau was obtained for the Friars Minor of Canterbury about 1300 and the gift was confirmed by Hugh of Hartlepool, then Provincial Minister.[8]

A fourteenth-century collection of treatises by Aristotle, Albertus Magnus, and others on natural science and alchemy, now in the Bodleian Library [9] belonged to " Friar John Bruyl of the Order of Friars Minor of the custody of London and the convent of Canterbury," who prefixed a table of contents and annotated the volume ; he was Warden of London in 1398.[10]

From an entry in Ch. Ch. Cant. MSS. Reg. O. fol. 404ʳ in the fifteenth century, it appears that the House possessed also a

---

[1] For this account of the books in the library I am indebted to Mr. A. G. Little.
[2] Brit. Mus. MSS. Royal, 3 C. XI.   [3] Nicolas, *Test. Vet.*, 761.
[4] Royal, 3 E. IX.   [5] *Ibid.* 3 D. II.
[6] *Ibid.* 2 D. XXIV; Cf. *New Palæogr. Soc. Facss.* pt. i. 1903, pl. 17, no. 3.
[7] Royal, 3 D. IV.   [8] Cotton Galba, E. XI.   [9] Digby, 153.
[10] Kingsford, *Grey Fr. Lond.* 56.

33

volume entitled *Notabilia super ecclesiasticam historiam et tripar-
titam cum extractionibus Willelmi Malmesburiensis*, having on the
back of the binding the letters "P.I.H." [1] The ten books which
Bishop Richard Martyn bequeathed to the House are not named
in his will.

Alexander Barclay (1475-1552), who was a poet, a scholar,
and a divine, as well as a voluminous writer, at some period of
his life joined the Canterbury Franciscans,[2] and possibly some of
his writings were to be found on the shelves of their library, his
most notable work being the translation of the *Shyp of Folys of
the World*, printed in 1509.

It is impossible now to ascertain the position of the library
at the Canterbury Friary. In London, in Newgate Street, a
magnificent library was built for the Minors by Sir Richard
Whittington in 1420-21, over the north alley of the Great
Cloister.[3] In Canterbury, the cloister was to the south of the
church, and if the library was built over the cloister, it must have
fully occupied one of the alleys, and would have consisted of
presses with shelves placed at right angles against the outer wall
of the alley, whilst the inner wall, pierced with windows and
glazed, looked into the Court, and was also fitted with presses
and shelves.

The scene, however, of the most interesting intellectual
activity of the friars in Canterbury of which we have information,
was not the Franciscan House but the Benedictine Priory of
Christ Church. Every metropolitan church was bound to provide
a school of theology for the instruction of priests and others in
Holy Scripture and pastoral duties. The monks of Christ Church
failed to carry out this obligation until the rise of Dominican
and Franciscan schools of theology stirred them to action. At
length in 1275 they established a school of theology and appointed a Franciscan, Friar William of Everel, as the first lecturer.
The monastic chronicler insists that the monks did it of their
own free will, but his comment suggests that they acted with
considerable misgivings: "This was unheard of in former times,
and what will be the result of this lecture and school, the future

[1] *Collect. Fr.* II, 9.　　　　　　　　[2] *Dict. Nat. Biog.*
[3] Kingsford, *Grey Fr. Lond.* 42, 170.

34

will show, since novelties produce quarrels."[1] It was perhaps an assertion of independence that during the archiepiscopate of the Dominican Kilwardby they chose a Franciscan as their lecturer.

How long William of Everel remained in office is unknown, but we can trace the later history of the lectureship through a series of letters preserved in the large collection of documents catalogued as Christ Church Letters in the Chapter Library[2] and the Register of Christ Church, now in the Cambridge University Library.[3] The earliest of these is an original letter from Friar W., Provincial Minister, to the Prior of Christ Church, written in the Provincial Chapter at Nottingham on Saturday after the Feast of the Assumption of the glorious Virgin. No year is given, but as William of Gainsborough was elected Provincial Minister by the Chapter at Cambridge in September 1285 and the Provincial Chapters in 1287, 1288 and 1289 are known to have been held in London, Lincoln, and Oxford respectively, the year of the Chapter at Nottingham was probably 1286 and the date of the letter 17 August, 1286. The gist of the letter is contained in the following sentence: " Although I have difficulty in sparing Friar Ralph de Wode-hay and greatly need his wisdom in other business, yet at your request I send him back, praying that his labour may bring forth abundant fruit in the hearts of your most studious sons." The next letter was sent by Prior Eastry to the Provincial Minister and dated 1 September, 1286. It is merely entered in the Register as a copy of the letter written to the friars in the preceding year with an additional clause apologizing for not writing before, "since we did not know that your General Chapter in England was being held earlier." The Provincial Chapter was often held on 8 September. The letter may imply that the letter of the Minister dated 17 August had not yet been received. The Register further contains a series of letters from the Prior of Christ Church to the Provincial Minister and Chapter of the Friars Minor between 1287 and 1298, asking them to continue

[1] *Gervas. Cantuar. Contin.* (*R.S.*) ii. 281.
[2] The relevant letters are printed in *Collect. Fr.* II, 4-8.
[3] MS. Ee. V, 31, ff. 24ᵛ, 28, 29, 34, 48ᵛ, 63, 66ᵛ, 78ᵛ.

35

Friar R. de Wydeheye in the office of lecturer to the monks: and an undated original letter of William of Gainsborough assures Prior Eastry that "Friar Ralph, as long as he remains, shall be obedient to you as he is to me." From these entries it is clear that Ralph de Wydeheye or Wodehay was lecturer to the monks from at least 1285 to 1298, and perhaps for longer, and that he was reappointed every year by the Provincial Minister and Provincial Chapter.

He was succeeded by at least one other friar, Robert of Fulham, who continued his lectures until 1314, when the monks wrote that "his teaching has so sweet an odour in the city of Canterbury, and has so fructified many of our congregation, his sedulous hearers, with the waters of Holy Scripture, that we regard them (i.e. his students) as fit to undertake the office of lecturer in our schools; we have therefore decided to appoint one of our fellow-monks to fill the post." [1]

Among the monks who were studying theology at Christ Church in Friar Ralph's time was Martin of Clive, an elderly and learned man who had previously been Regent Master in Arts.[2] He possessed a considerable library of theological books, which on his death in 1301 passed to the library of the Priory.[3] We may infer that Friar Ralph gave advanced lectures on theology, probably " with disputations," [4] as in the Universities.

Seven years after the friars had ceased to preside over the monastic school of theology, Archbishop Reynolds instructed the monks to provide suitable accommodation for the lecturer; hitherto he had had no study and was compelled to do his work in the Infirmary.[5] It is possible that the friar-lecturers lodged at the Grey Friars : but it is more likely that they resided in the Priory and put up with the inconveniences.

The relations of the friars to the Priory of Christ Church seem to have been fairly friendly if not very close. A Brother Solomon of Ripple stirred up the people against the Prior in a Sunday sermon on Sandwich Marsh in 1323, but he was a monk

[1] Little, *Grey Fr. Oxf.* 66.
[2] Ch. Ch. Letters, R. IV, 13 : *Collect. Fr.* II, 7.
[3] James, *Anc. Libraries of Canterbury and Dover*, pp. 131-3, 172, 535.
[4] Cf. *Eccleston*, ed. Little, p. 63.   [5] *Collect. Fr.* II, 8.

of St. Austin's Abbey.[1]   Peter of Bologna, the Franciscan bishop of Corbava in Hungary, who acted as suffragan in Canterbury and other dioceses till his death in January 1332, was evidently a *persona grata* to Prior Eastry.[2]   And another suffragan bishop, Friar Richard Martyn, was a brother and benefactor of the Priory of Christ Church.[3]

The rent of 3s. which the friars agreed to pay in 1294[4] was a source of trouble.   The friars having neglected to pay it, the monks withdrew an annual grant which they were accustomed to make to the friars.   Queen Isabella, widow of Edward II, about 1342-3, wrote to request a renewal of the grant, but Prior Robert Hathbrand, explaining the circumstances, refused to comply with the Queen's request.   His letter reads as follows :—

To the most noble lady the Lady Isabel, etc., her humble and devout chaplains the Prior and Monks of the Church of Canterbury, recommend themselves prepared to do all her good pleasure.

Most honourable Lady, we received your gracious letter of 24 July, by the hands of Thomas de Stourton your servant, asking us to give to those good religious men, the Friars Minor of Canterbury, our alms (which for a time have been withheld) in the same manner as we formerly did, and this the more courteously, because of your request.   And, very gracious lady, because you have not been told the cause of the withdrawal of the said alms, if it please you we let you know that the same Friars have enclosed in their Precinct a considerable piece of ground which is charged with a rent to our Church, so that we cannot enter to distrain for the arrears which are of large amount ; which enclosure in time to come, unless they do what in justice they ought to do, might end in the disherison of us and our Church, a thing to which our conscience neither can consent, nor ought it to do so, wherefore since that time our charity towards them has not been so ready as aforetime. But, very noble lady, out of reverence to you and your request, we will give the said alms to the Friars (this being purely a matter of favour), the right of our Church being always reserved, provided they act towards us and our Church as they are bound by justice to do ; and we beg that you will please to command them so to act.   May God keep you, lady, and grant you long life.   Written in our Chapter the 27th July.[5]

However both the great Benedictine Monasteries in Canterbury classed the friars among the poor and gave them alms.[6]

St. Francis wished his brethren to be humble helpers of the parish priests, but as the friars themselves became to a large

[1] *Lit. Cant.* I, 110.   [2] *Ibid.* I, 300-1, 421 ; cf. Kingsford, *Grey Fr. Lond.* 72.
[3] See below, Appendix III.   [4] See above, p. 19.
[5] Ch. Ch. Cant. MSS. Reg. L., fol. 78 : printed in *Lit. Cant.* (*R.S.*) II, 263.
[6] See Ch. IV.

extent an Order of priests, and, as their papal privileges grew, disputes and rivalries inevitably arose between them and the local ecclesiastical authorities. Canterbury was no exception to the general rule. The Franciscan Archbishop Pecham, who had been Provincial Minister before his elevation to the throne of St. Austin, naturally took the part of the friars. Thus in July, 1287, he instructed the clergy of his diocese to call in the assistance of holy men specially deputed to preach and hear confessions,[1] i.e. the friars : and on 2 December, 1287, he ordered the Archdeacon of Canterbury to forbid rectors, vicars, and curates to assert that the friars had not power to hear confessions and grant absolution, and declared that the friars were generally more learned and more saintly than the seculars.[2] Boniface VIII settled this as well as other quarrels between the regulars and seculars by the Bull " Super Cathedram " in 1300, which required that friars must be licensed by the bishop before they could hear confessions in the diocese. Accordingly in 1300 Archbishop Winchelsey licensed eight Grey Friars to hear confessions in the diocese of Canterbury,[3] and Archbishop Reynolds in 1323 licensed the Warden Friar Robert of St. Albans, Friars Nicholas of Clive, Alan of Bourne, and William Venables, to hear confessions and to preach in the place of four friars who had been transferred elsewhere ; and the statement is added : " Their custodian at Canterbury admits that there are eight others of their Order now residing at Canterbury so licensed besides the aforesaid four." [4]

The supply of suitable friars at Canterbury seems to have been inadequate to fill the gaps caused by the Black Death in 1349; for in November 1358, Archbishop Islip admitted five Friars Minor of the convent of Oxford—namely John of Withingham, John of Cowley, John of Horwood, Roger of Nottingham, and John Walsch'—and three Friars Minor of the Convent of Cambridge—namely John of Walsham, Robert of Sutton, and Roger of Snoring, together with two Cambridge Friars Preachers—to preach in the diocese of Canterbury.[5]

Within fifty years of their coming to Canterbury the Minors

---

[1] *Reg. Epist. Peckham* (R.S.) III, p. 949.   [2] *Ibid.* 952.
[3] *Ann. Mon.* (R.S.) IV, 546.   [4] Lambeth MSS. Reg. Reynolds, fol. 249ᵛ.
[5] Lambeth MSS. Reg. Islip, fol. 144ᵛ.

had gained the entire confidence of the great and highly placed as well as the humble and poor; Sir Gregory de Rokesley, Mayor of London, 1274-81, and again 1284-5, who died in 1291, was a great benefactor to the Minors of London: in his will[1] he gave direction that the residue of his estates in London, Canterbury, and Rochester were to be given to the poor, and that the Wardens of the Minors in London and in Canterbury were to be consulted as to the disposal of them.

Their church at Canterbury (as all other churches) was "Sanctuary," and occasionally it is recorded amongst the Muniments of the Realm that felons fled thither for refuge. In 1305[2] one William of Gerberg, a Knight, was indicted before the Coroners of the County of Norfolk that he had procured three men to kill another, of which indictment he was afraid, and fled to the Church of the Minors at Canterbury and remained there for full half a year.

On 8 February, 1338, pardon was granted to John Atte Noke of Newington, and John de Bromesdon, Friars Minor of Canterbury, for the rescue of Thomas Sauvage of Sharstede and John Wydour, felons adjudged to death at Canterbury by Geoffrey le Scrope and other justices, while on their way to execution; and on 28 February, John Nichol, Rector of All Saints, Canterbury, and Stephen Lucas, Rector of Oteringdenne (Otterden), had pardon for their part in rescuing the same felons.[3]

In the last half of the fifteenth century signs of change may be detected in the house of the Grey Friars. In an undated list of licensed confessors (*penitenciarii*) (*c.* 1490?) only two Friars Minor—William Knight, the warden, and Thomas Cok are mentioned as against five Dominicans.[4] This may imply a decrease in the numbers of the house. The friars seem to have retained their popularity among the laity. In 1481-2 the Mayor and his brethren " with other venerable men of the city " granted to the Friars Minor 6s. 8d. in relief of pavage,[5] and prominent

---

[1] *Cal. of Wills Court of Husting, London,* I, 99.
[2] *Year Books of Edward I (R.S.)* 33 Edw. I, 55.
[3] *Cal. Pat. Rolls,* 12 Edw. III, Vol. 1338-40, pp. 19, 22.
[4] Ch. Ch. MSS. Reg. N., fol. 172.
[5] Bunce's MS. Extracts from Canterbury Accounts, I, p. 28.

citizens remembered them in their wills, though it may be noted that few bequests from secular clerks are known during this period. Among other bequests are several to individual friars.[1] Richard Martyn was evidently at the date of his will (1498) living in private apartments in the convent, with a separate kitchen, in considerable state—and his married brother, John Martyn, was provided with lodgings at the Grey Friars.[2] Richard Martyn was, however, a bishop and enjoyed exceptional privileges. More significant is the licence granted by Pius II to Thomas Cok, Friar Minor of Canterbury, on 27 September, 1459, to hold a benefice and to wear his habit under a mantle of decent colour.[3] Was he ashamed of his habit?

Another characteristic of the period is the considerable influx of foreign friars which took place between 1450 and 1470, from Strasbourg, Coblenz, Cologne, and the Low Countries. The explanation may possibly be that these were Conventual Friars ejected from their houses by the Observants and seeking a fresh home among their Conventual brethren. But Canterbury itself became an Observant house before the end of the century.

During the early part of the fifteenth century there was a movement within the Franciscan Order for the strict observance of the Rule of St. Francis, as during the previous hundred years much of the old Franciscan simplicity of life had been lost, the Minorites having become landowners and holding property which the piety of their predecessors had won for them. Certain of the more enthusiastic of the brethren abroad, headed by Friar Bernardino of Siena, determined to return to the primitive life, calling themselves Friars Observants; they followed the *Regula Bullata* with the modifications of Popes Nicholas III and Clement V—not the Primitive Rule be it understood. They denounced the easy going and luxury loving friars who dwelt in such comfort as the fifteenth century provided, whom they called Conventuals. Both parties attempted to obtain the support of Pope Eugenius IV who had been elected in 1431; he had formerly been a member of a reformed monastery, and was a

<hr />

[1] See Appendix III.   [2] *Ibid.*   [3] *Cal Pap. L.* X, 563.

40

favourer of the Observants to such an extent, that they were said " to swarm in Rome like rats." [1]

The idea of the Pope was to form the Minorites into a powerful arm of the Holy See, and in this he proved successful. He died in 1447, but had already granted to the Observants the privilege of electing two Vicars-General of their own (for the Cismontane and Ultramontane Families respectively) [2] whom the Minister-General had to confirm but over whom he exercised no authority; each Province of Observant Friars also elected the Provincial Vicar, and held Provincial Chapters, or Congregations as they were called, independent of the Conventuals.

This aggravated rather than allayed dissension in the Order. Many attempts were made by successive Popes to re-establish unity, but, except for some brief intervals, the Bull of Eugenius IV regulated the relations between the two branches of the Order until 1517. In that year Leo X reversed the relations between the two branches : the title of Minister was henceforth confined to the Order of Friars Minor of the strict Observance, while the heads of the Conventuals were called Master-General and Masters-Provincial and had to obtain Confirmation from the Minister-General and Ministers-Provincial of the Observants.

The constitutions governing the Ultramontane Family of the Observants (to which England ultimately belonged) were issued by the General Chapter of Barcelona in 1451. These provided for the election of guardians by convents, the election of Provincial Vicars and the Vicar-General by the (annual) Provincial Chapter and the (triennial) General Chapters respectively. The most marked feature was the insistence on short terms of office, which were not to exceed three years. This was in contrast with the contemporary practice of the Conventuals (among whom the Prelates generally held office for long periods) and helped to save the Order from stagnation. The Observants were introduced into England by Edward IV in 1482, and their first House was established at Greenwich with the approval of Pope Sixtus IV

[1] Poggio's *Dialogus contra hypocrisim*, quoted by Creighton in *History of the Papacy*, Vol. II, p. 272.
[2] According to present-day usage Cismontane denotes south of the Alps, Ultramontane, north of the Alps.

and dedicated to[1] the Blessed Virgin, St. Francis and All Saints. Henry VII confirmed the grant, and founded an Observant Friary there to consist of a Warden and twelve brethren at the least.

There were never more than six houses of Observant Friars[2] in this country; Greenwich, Richmond, Canterbury, Southampton, Newcastle, and Newark. Two of these were royal foundations connected with royal palaces. Three were transferred from the Conventuals to the Observants by royal command issued to the Provincial Chapter in 1498.

"This same yere in August," notes the author of the Chronicle of the Grey Friars of London, "was the ij[de] prouincialle chapter of the Freer Minores in London. And there beganne the Observanttes, and came with the kynges letteres and commandment for sertayne placis, and so beganne with Newcastelle, Cantorbery and Sowth-hamton."[3]

There is nothing to show why these three houses were selected. They were, however, all in fairly close contact with the continent, and the Observant movement had as yet attracted few recruits in England and was largely dependent on foreign accessions. The history of the transfer of the Canterbury house is even more obscure than that of Newcastle or Southampton; there appears to be no mention of it in the City Records or in the archiepiscopal registers. Probably some Observant Friars were imported from abroad to introduce Observant discipline and principles, but the house had no property the holding of which was inconsistent with those principles, and it is likely that the inmates accommodated themselves to the change.

Down to 1498 the English Observants had been under the direction of a commissary first of the Vicar-General of the Ultramontane Observants, and then of the Provincial Vicar of Cologne; now England, having enough houses and friars, was accorded the privileges of a province by the General Chapter of the Ultramontane Family at Malines, 19 May, 1499.[4]

The Observant Friars were active preachers in the neighbourhood; thus the corporation of New Romney paid 6d. for the expenses of the Brothers Observant in the house of Edward

[1] Arch. Journal, XXIII, 57. "Introduction of the Observant Friars into England," by A. G. Little (Proc. of Brit. Acad. XI.)
[2] L. and P. Hen. VIII. I, 5737, 5738.
[3] Mon. Franc. II, 182.   [4] Anal. Fr. II, 521.

Wodell, when they came to preach in the church of St. Nicholas in 1506, and in 1517-18 gave 3s. 4d. in alms to the Observants of Canterbury.[1] Among their benefactors were several secular priests, and a considerable proportion of the gifts recorded are gifts in kind.[2] The Observants continued to enjoy the royal patronage, and in 1514 Henry VIII wrote to Pope Leo X that "he could not sufficiently express his admiration for their strict adherence to poverty, their sincerity, charity, and devotion. No Order battled against vice more assiduously; none were more active in keeping Christ's fold."[3]

[1] *Hist. MSS. Com.* Rep. V, 550, 552.   [2] See Chapter IV.
[3] *L. and P. Hen. VIII*, I, no. 4871.

CHAPTER IV.

THE BENEFACTORS OF THE HOUSE.

THE donors of the site and some of the earlier benefactors have already been mentioned. It is remarkable that few gifts from Henry III, a great benefactor to the Friars generally and markedly to the Dominicans of Canterbury, are recorded to the Grey Friars of this house. In the *Liberate Rolls*, 10 March, 1239, is the order : " Deliver to the Friars Minor of Canterbury ten marks (£6 13s. 4d.) of the King's gift for maintenance." Apart from this, fifteen cartloads of fuel in 1241, 50s. to buy wood in 1246, and six beech trees in 1272 seem to be the only grants from Henry III mentioned in the Public Records.[1]

Edward I gave them fuel in 1278 and 1293,[2] and made them grants for pittances when staying in Canterbury. Some of these have already been referred to as showing the numbers of friars in the house at various times. No doubt the King and Queen gave gifts to the friars when staying in Canterbury on their return from Crusade in the summer of 1274, but the only gifts on this occasion which have yet been discovered are contained in the Wardrobe Accounts of Henry, the infant son of Edward I : " On Thursday [2 August, 1274] at the Friars Preachers as an offering 3d. . . . On the following Wednesday [8 August] at the Friars Minor of Canterbury 3d. Item given to the poor at the door of the Church 2½d." [3] Princess Mary, daughter of Edward I, gave them 10s. when on pilgrimage in Canterbury in 1302.[4] And King John of France when he passed through

---

[1] *Liberate Rolls*, 25 Hen. III, m. 5, 30 Hen. III, m. 9; *Close Roll*, 56 Hen. III, m. 7.
[2] *Close Rolls*, 6 Edw. I, m. 3; 21 Edw. I, m. 5.
[3] *Bulletin of the John Rylands Library*, VII, 419.
[4] P.R.O. Exch. Accts. 362 (14).

Canterbury on his return home from captivity, on 4 July 1360, gave 25 nobles (£8 6s. 8d.) to the Grey Friars.[1]

Royal alms were few and far between. The Canterbury Friars received no regular payments either from the Exchequer or from the City. They had to depend for their ordinary maintenance on the produce of their gardens, voluntary alms and the results of house to house begging, bequests, payments for masses, and mortuary fees.

Alms in kind are not often recorded except in monastic accounts. Thus the Treasurer of St. Austin's Abbey in 1432 accounts for "three quarters of corn given to the three Orders of Mendicant Friars in Canterbury," and similar entries are frequent (e.g. in 1469-70).[2] Another undated and fragmentary roll of the fifteenth century records "payment for three bullocks given in alms to the Friars Minor of Canterbury this year, 48s. ; and for sheep given to the same in alms this year, 16s."[3] The extant accounts also show that the monks of Christ Church gave the friars a quarter of corn yearly during the fourteenth century; the grant was discontinued in 1343 owing to the dispute already referred to, but it reappears in 1360 and the following years.[4]

The churches and churchyards of the Minors were favourite places for interment, though they did not possess the right of sepulture till 1227, and even then Pope Gregory IX only granted permission for the members of the Order themselves to be buried in their own precincts.[5] Permission for the burial of lay-folk was not given till 1250, when Pope Innocent IV allowed it, provided that the rights and privileges of the church where the deceased would otherwise have been buried were preserved,[6] and lastly, the Bull " Super Cathedram " in 1300,[7] settled that the friars should have the right to bury lay-folk, provided that they gave to the Parish Priest one-fourth part of all burial fees.

[1] *Gentleman's Mag.* Sept. 1859, p. 277.
[2] Treasurer's Accts. of St. Austin's Abbey: Ch. Ch. Cant. MS. Roll. Cabinet CC. ; MS. F.I.I. fols. 10v, 23v. .
[3] St. Augustine's College, MS. Roll.
[4] Ch. Ch. Cant. MSS. Almoners Accts. for years 1321-2, 1324-5, 1327-8, 1336, 1337, 1360, 1361-2, 1368-9, 1372, 1373.
[5] *Bull. Franc.* I, p. 31.
[6] *Ibid.* p. 537. Cf. Little, *Studies,* 108.
[7] *Bull. Franc.* IV, p. 498 : incorporated in Canon Law, *Clem.* Lib. 3, Tit. 7, De Sepulturis, Cap 2.

Thus was settled a controversy with the Secular Clergy which for nearly eighty years had raged round the three important matters of (1) the right of the Friars to bury their own brethren in their own precinct, (2) the right to bury lay-folk therein, and (3) the right to retain the mortuary fees in the latter case.

In Canterbury not only citizens, but many persons of rank were desirous of burial in a place which by its peculiar sanctity had become fashionable. The following list of burials in the Grey Friars is based on the list in Weever's *Ancient Funerall Monuments* (p. 238), which was Hasted's authority (some corrections and identifications have been added) :—

Sir William Balliol, 1313 ; Bartholomew of Badlesmere, Lord of Leeds Castle, who was hanged for rebellion at Blean in April, 1322 ; his son Sir Giles of Badlesmere, kt., who died 20 June, 1338 ;[1] Elizabeth, Lady of Chilham—probably sister of Giles of Badlesmere ; Sir William Manston,[2] kt., perhaps the sheriff of Kent in 1435 ; Sir Roger Manston his brother ; Sir John[3] Brockhull, kt., 1382, to be buried at the chancel door near his first wife Edith ; and their son Sir Thomas Brockhull,[4] and his wife Joan ; Sir Falcon Payferer or Sir Fulk Peyforer, kt. ; Sir Thomas Dayner or D'Aymer, kt. ; Lady Alice of Maryms or de Marinis ; Lady Candlin ; "Sir Alan Pennington of . . . in the county of Lancaster, kt., who coming from the wars beyond seas died in this City"; Lady Ladrie or Audrey of Valence ; Sir William Trussell, kt. ; Sir Bartholomew Ashburnham, kt. ; Sir John Montenden or Mottenden, "knight and a Friar of this house."

In the Appendix will be found abstracts of the wills of the following persons who were, or desired to be, buried in the Grey Friars' Church or cemetery: Thomas Somer (1463), Thomas Barton (1477), Thomas Ketcham (1478), Richard Annesley (1484), Margaret Cherche (1486), John Forde (1487), Milo Denne (1491), Hamo Bele (1492), mayor of Canterbury, and

---

[1] Gibbons, *Early Lincoln Wills*, p. 6.
[2] Of Manston in the Isle of Thanet.
[3] Weever and Hasted call him Thomas ; but see his will in Nicolas, *Test. Vet.* 115.
[4] Commissioner of Array in Kent, Captain of Merk Castle, Calais, 1382, etc., see *Cal. Pat. Rolls*, Ric. II.

Elizabeth his wife; John Baker (1495), John Martyn (1496), Richard Martyn (1498), Henry Ramsey (1500), Thomas Colman (1503), John Morys (1507), Arnold Fromvar or Fromere (1514), Peter William (1517), Alexander Elyothe, priest (1524), Sybilla Lewknor (1528), George Chadworth (1530), rector of St. Nicholas, Ryngewold; Katherine Downe (1531), Anne Culpeper (1532), John Dibden (1538). To these may be added Elizabeth Master (1522).[1]

These two lists furnish striking contrasts; the earlier one contains the names of nobles or of members of county families. These classes are almost unrepresented in the later list; from the middle of the fifteenth century onwards the burials recorded are almost entirely those of citizens of Canterbury. The fact that two secular priests in the sixteenth century desired to be buried among the Friars suggests that the Observants maintained friendly relations with the clergy.

The Minors received a large number of bequests from persons of all ranks: the bequests were generally accompanied by a stipulation that masses should be said for the soul of the deceased. In 1253 Richard Wych, Bishop of Chichester, left them 20s. besides a book.[2] They received 40s. from Archbishop Winchelsey[3] in 1313, 40s. from Archbishop Reynolds[4] in 1327, and bequests from Archbishops Stafford in 1348,[5] Courtney in 1396,[6] and Arundel in 1414.[7] John Rogg of Romney, in 1374, left an instrument granting leave to his executors to transfer to the Franciscan and Austin Friars of Canterbury a bequest of 40 marks to secular chaplains to say masses in Romney Church, owing to the scarcity of chaplains in Romney Marsh. John Buckingham, Bishop of Lincoln, who died at Meister Omers in the Precincts on 10 March, 1399, and founded a chantry in the cathedral, left 20s. to the Friars Minor here.[8]

Other benefactors were Philip de Turvill, canon of Lichfield,

---

[1] Hasted, Kent, IV, 447.
[2] Chichester Epis. Reg. Rede E., p. 176, Sussex Archæol. Collections, I, 164-92, Nicolas, Test. Vet., 761.
[3] Sede Vacante Wills (Kent Records), pp. 64, 69, 74, 84.
[4] Ibid.   [5] Ibid.
[6] Arch. Cant. Vol. XXIII, pp. 65-6 (5 marcs).
[7] Ibid. p. 34.   [8] Ibid. p. 100.

1337;[1] Elizabeth de Burgh, Lady of Clare, 1360;[2] Walter de Berney, 1377;[3] Sir Richard atte Lease, kt., 1393;[4] William St. Nicholas of St. Nicholas in Thanet, 1396;[5] John Tyece of Canterbury, 1400;[6] John Vagge, rector of St. Martin's Church, Canterbury, 1402;[7] William Scott of Scots Hall (sheriff of Kent), 1433;[8] Richard Fawkener of Warehorn, 1442;[9] Valentine Baret of Perry Court, in Preston next Faversham, in 1440;[10] William Byllyngton of All Saints, Canterbury, who died 21 November, 1444, and left £10 to the Minorites "to the building of le Dortour";[11] William Woodland of Holy Cross, Canterbury, who left £5 for the repair of the church and 5 marks for the repair of the dormitory in 1450.[12] William Harry of St. Martin's in 1461 left the friars 2s. 6d. for thirty masses, at the rate of 1d. for a mass.[13] Richard Tilley in 1485 left a small sum;[14] William Bochard or Roper, in 1488, left the warden 20d. and each friar 4d.;[15] and Agnes Bochard, his widow, in 1492, left 6s. 8d. to the friars and 8d. to the Guild of Corpus Christi in their Church.[16]

Among the points illustrated by the wills from which extracts are printed in the Appendix, we may draw attention to the following.[17] The largest bequest is £20 left by Roger Ridley, formerly mayor, in 1471. The largest bequest for the reparation of church and buildings is that of 20 marcs made by Edmund Minot in 1488. Of the £10 left by Thomas Somer in 1463 only the remainder was to go to beautifying the church after 6s. 8d. had been paid to each friar of the house. The wills contain a number of gifts to individual friars. Thus Friar Thomas Cok was left a maser by William Haute in 1462 and 20s. by Bishop Richard Martyn in 1485. William Knight, sometime warden, received a bequest of 20s. in 1486. John Darell, Sompnour, in 1496 left 8d.

[1] *Arch. Cant.* Vol. XXIII, p. 121. [2] Nichols, *Royal Wills*, 23.
[3] *Norf. Antiq. Miscell.* I, 400; Sharpe, *Cal. of Wills*, II, 205.
[4] P.C.C. Rous., f. 22. [5] Ch. Ch. MSS. Reg. G., f. 265.
[6] Cant. City Archives, Wills and Deeds, f. 3.
[7] See Appendix III. [8] *Arch. Cant.* X. 261.
[9] *Ibid.* XI. [10] *Trans. of Monumental Brass Soc.* VI.
[11] Lambeth MSS. Reg. Stafford, f. 125.
[12] Hasted, *Kent*, IV, 447. [13] Appendix III.
[14] Cant. City Archives, Wills and Deeds, f. 18.
[15] Appendix III. [16] *Ibid.*
[17] Those throwing light on the interior of the Church have been noted in Chapter II.

to the warden, 4d. to each friar and 20d. to his brother Ralph Darell, a friar of this house, besides 16 bushels of wheat. Another remarkable bequest in kind is that of William Bigge, miller, and mayor of Canterbury, who left the large sum of £10 13s. 4d. to the Friars Minor to sing masses in St. Peter's Church—this sum to be paid in ale. Another benefactor, William Whithale, provides for friars being sent to Whitstable to celebrate for his soul. Among the bequests of Bishop Martyn (1498) were several legacies in kind in addition to the gifts of church ornaments and books, elsewhere referred to : his wheat stored at the Grey Friars was to be divided between the friars and the poor ; every friar was to have a new habit of russet ; his great bed in the Chapel Chamber with all apparel and, hangings was left to the Grey Friars' House ; two other beds, with silver plate, chest with two locks, and " all my nets " were left to his sister-in-law and his nephew ; and his boat was to go to Master John Diggs, probably a descendant of the founder and himself a benefactor of the friars.

Bishop Martyn, though his will was made shortly after the transfer of the house to the Observants, belonged to the old order of things. The earliest legacy to the Observant House as such was 20s. left by Henry Ramsey in 1500, and it is noteworthy that the handling of it was entrusted not to the friars but to the Rector of St. Andrew's on their behalf.[1] Thomas Colman, in 1503, desired to be buried in the cemetery and left 20d. for that purpose—perhaps the smallest legacy for a burial on record.[2] John Bakke (1500), and Elizabeth, wife of John Hale, alderman (1506), left them small sums ; and many bequests of varying amounts, chiefly from citizens of Canterbury, will be found in Appendix III.[3] By far the greatest benefactor was Henry VII, who in his will left them 100 marcs (£66 13s. 4d.) and entrusted £200 for their use to the Prior of Christ Church.[4] They received £13 6s. 8d. from Henry VIII for saying daily masses for the late king in 1509.[5]

---

[1] See Appendix III ; cf. the reference to the friar's proctor in the will of Elinore Hawes, 1511 ; *ibid.* (A somewhat similar provision occurs in the will of W. Whithale, 1474.)
[2] *Ibid.* [3] Cant. City Archives, Wills and Deeds, ff. 18, 21.
[4] Astle, *Will of Henry VII*, p. 30. [5] *L. and P. Hen. VIII*, II, 1445.

Gifts and legacies in kind were a marked feature of the history of the Observant House. Elizabeth of York, Queen of Henry VII, in 1502, paid to "my lady Bray"[1] £6 13s. 4d. for fifty-two barrels of beer delivered to the Friars Observant of Canterbury for a whole year.[2] John Diggs left them bread and victuals in 1503; Stephen Barrett, corn and salt in 1504; Gerard Johnson, beer-brewer, three barrels of double beer and three of single beer in 1506. Giles Talbot, parson of St. Martin's, left them corn in 1524.[3] Sir John Rudstone, kt., and alderman of London, in 1530, bequeathed to them "one long grey woollen cloth for their habits," price 5 marcs.[4] John Thomlyn, priest, left them wheat and malt in 1531.[5]

The large legacy of £5 6s. 8d. which another priest, Alexander Elyothe, left in 1524 for "a friar to sing masses for my soul for one year"[6] cannot be regarded as a gift to an individual. On the other hand the Canterbury friars received from Henry Hatche of Faversham, in 1533, besides a legacy of 5 marcs, an annual grant of 15s.,[7] which seems hardly consistent with strict Observant principles.

So far as the evidence goes, it seems to show that legacies from secular priests were more numerous, legacies from the gentry in the surrounding country less numerous, in the Observant than in the Conventual period. A legacy from Sir John Roper of Eltham, in 1524,[8] brings the Canterbury Observants into distant connexion with Sir Thomas More. The will of Sibylla Lewknor, 1528, implies that the ancient connexion of the Friary with the Scotts of Scott Hall was still kept up.[9] From Lord Darcy the friars received a gift of 5 marcs in 1526;[10] and Lord Lisle, in 1534 (a black year for the English Observants), authorized the collection of money at Calais for "the Grey Friars of Canterbury who have no lands or rents."[11] A legacy of 40s. from James Diggs

---

[1] Wife of Sir Reginald Bray?
[2] *Privy Purse Expenses of Eliz. of York*, ed. Nicolas, p. 57.
[3] Consistory Court Wills, Canterbury: see Appendix III.
[4] MS. Harl. 1231, f. 2v.   [5] Appendix III.
[6] *Ibid.*   [7] Nicolas, *Test Vet.*, 662.
[8] *Arch. Cant.* II, 169.
[9] *See* Appendix. A legacy of 10s. from William Lewies of Ash, in 1526, may be mentioned, *Arch. Cant.*, XXXVI, 52.
[10] *L. and P. Hen. VIII*, IV, 2527.   [11] *Ibid.* VII, 1620.

of Barham,[1] may imply that the bond between the Friary and its thirteenth-century founder was maintained to the end.

A form for the admission of persons to the privileges of the Order of St. Francis written in 1479, by John, Warden of the Friars at Canterbury, in accordance with a recent grant from the Franciscan Pope Sixtus IV, shows that letters of fraternity were issued by the House, but a blank is left for the names;[2] and no completed letter of fraternity of this House has been found. It may also be noticed that no benefactors of the House are described in their wills as members of the Third Order.

[1] P.C.C. 17 Alenger.   [2] Bodl. Charter 153*.

CHAPTER V.

FRIARS RICHE AND RISBY, AND THE HOLY MAID OF KENT.

A PROVINCIAL Chapter was held in Canterbury in the year 1532,[1] at which the celebrated Friar William Peto (afterwards Cardinal Peto), was present. On Sunday, 1 May, before leaving Greenwich for Canterbury to attend this Chapter, Friar Peto preached before King Henry VIII, on the matter of the divorce, and took for his text: "Where the dogs licked the blood of Naboth, even there shall they lick thy blood, O King," and there can be no doubt that during the Provincial Chapter the question of the divorce was discussed by the friars assembled; and the Holy Maid of Kent, then a nun of St. Sepulchre's, Canterbury, was possibly interviewed. The story of Elizabeth Barton cannot fully be told here, but the complicity of two of her friends Friar Hugh Riche, the late[2] warden of the Canterbury House, and Friar Richard Risby, the then warden, does certainly concern us. The whole story of Elizabeth Barton can best be studied in Lambard's *Perambulations in Kent*, written in 1570, but not published till 1576; his account is based on a tract which was written by Edward Thwaites, a Kentish gentleman of note, entitled *A Miraculous work, of late done at Court of Street, in Kent, published to the devoute People of this tyme, for their spiritual consolation*, 1527, which according to J. R. Smith in *Bibliotheca Cantiana* was so extraordinarily rare that he had not been able to trace a single copy. The reason is not far to seek, as in the Act of Attainder of the Holy Maid, the destruction of every copy of this work was ordered, under pain of fine and imprisonment. There is also a MS. entitled "The Revelations of Elizabeth

---

[1] Chr. Davenport, *Hist. Min.*, 51.
[2] Act of Attainder, 1533-4 in the *Statutes of the Realm*, Vol. III, p. 449.

Barton" in the Public Record Office quoted by Froude in his history, Vol. I, p. 324, which throws much light on the proceedings; but best of all are the accounts given in Cardinal Gasquet's *Henry VIII, and the English Monasteries* (1888), and Mr. A. D. Cheney's Paper on "The Holy Maid of Kent" read before the Royal Historical Society, 17 March, 1904, and printed in their *Transactions* (New Series, Vol. XVIII (1904)).

Elizabeth Barton, originally a serving maid at Aldington, was an hysterical and extremely neurotic young woman, evidently at times on the verge of religious mania. After a good deal of religious excitement she became a nun of St. Sepulchre's Benedictine Convent, Canterbury. Here she lived for some years, the discipline and quietude of the religious life being conducive to a return to a more normal condition of mind. She eventually, however, let herself go, and in addition to a reputation for extreme holiness of life she claimed to possess supernatural powers. In this she was evidently aided and abetted by those who should have known better, namely Dr. Bocking, the cellarer of Christ Church, Canterbury, John Dering, a monk there, Friar Hugh Riche, the late warden of the Grey Friars, and Friar Risby, the present warden of the Canterbury House. All these and others,[1] including Richard Master, the Vicar of Aldington, and Henry Gold, a secular priest, became involved in a political movement, which in those days was considered and punished as treason. A Bill of Attainder was passed in 1534, and Elizabeth Barton and five of her companions were executed on 20 April that year. Until recently all the seven persons named above, were supposed to have suffered death at Tyburn, but researches during the last few years prove that at least one escaped. Burnet says[2] Friar Hugh Riche, the late warden, probably died in prison shortly

---

[1] Friar Christopher Warener, the Dominican recluse or anchorite in the Blackfriars at Canterbury had been visited by Elizabeth Barton, "because he was a prisoner"; this came to Cromwell's knowledge and he tried to induce the friar to incriminate the nun; but like many another anchorite or hermit, who had retired from the world, its pomps and vanities, he was sufficiently worldly-wise to declare that "he was never of counsel with the nun, had never seen her in a trance, nor heard her say a word against the king, except that should the marriage with Anne go forward it would turn to great trouble." He also declared that these matters were a great hindrance to his contemplation, etc., and thus escaped the meshes woven by Cromwell. *L. and P. Hen. VIII*, Vol. VI, 1333, 1336, 1381.

[2] Pocock's *Burnet's Hist. of the Reformation*, Vol. I, p. 252.

before the execution, but whether or not, he was buried along with the Holy Maid and his brother Friar Risby at the Grey Friars Church [1] in London. But Burnet is in error; on the very day, 20 April, 1534, after the execution, John Hussee,[2] writing to Lord Lisle, says, "This day the nonne of Kent w[t]. ii frers obs(ervan)ts ii monks and one secular prest were drawne from the tow[r]. to tiborne and there hanged and hedyd. God if it be is plez[r]. have m(er)cy on theyr sowlls." The only one to escape was the Vicar of Aldington, Richard Master, who had offered a bribe to Cromwell of two gold crowns,[3] and the bribe had been accepted. In proof of this, though Stow's *Annals* and Strype's *Memorials* state that he was executed along with the others, and modern historians, including Cardinal Gasquet, have naturally accepted this statement, a reference to *The Depositions of witnesses taken before Master Robert Collens, L.L.B., Commissary-General*,[4] in the Consistory Court Books in the Library of the Dean and Chapter at Canterbury, under date 7 November, 1550, will show that he was alive in that year and asked to be relieved of a sentence of excommunication which had been pronounced against him for not complying with the order to abolish the altars in his church; his petition was granted on condition that he carried out the order within one week, and certified to the Court that he had done so. Again under date 11 December, 1552, the same Richard Master, Parson of Aldington, signs the Inventory of Church Goods [5] of the Parish of Aldington, Kent; but as his name does not occur under Aldington, in the "Visitation of Archdeacon Harpsfield taken in 1557," [6] we must conclude that he died somewhere between 1552 and 1557, and so at least survived for eighteen years after the Act of Attainder had passed sentence upon him.

Doubtless the two gold crowns were only part of the gift; he was for a country parson a wealthy man, as appears from the

[1] *Grey Friars Chronicle*, Camden Soc., p. 37.
[2] *L. and P. Hen. VIII*, Vol. VII, 522; cf. Lisle Papers, Vol. V, 95.
[3] *L. and P. Hen. VIII*, VI, No. 1666.
[4] Rev. C. E. Woodruff in *Arch. Cant.* Vol. XXXI, p. 95.
[5] P.R.O. "Church Goods, Kent, temp. Edw. VI, 3/13 to 3/45."
[6] Ch. Ch. Cant. MS. X.Y.Z.

inventory of his household goods published by Froude in Vol. I, of his History, copied from a MS. in the P.R.O.

Cardinal Gasquet says that Father Thomas Bourchier,[1] who joined the Franciscan Order in 1557 at Greenwich, and would therefore have known the details, declares that the lives of the two brethren, Fathers Risby and Riche, were twice offered to them, if they would accept Henry as supreme Head of the English Church. This offer was of course rejected, and those who know what executions at that time at Tyburn signified, can estimate the manner of the deaths of these six persons. They were first hanged at a "pair of gallows" with a drop of only about three or four feet, a stout rope was used and arranged in such a manner that death by strangulation was impossible; they were then cut down whilst alive, ripped open, their bowels and other viscera drawn out, and their hearts rubbed in their mouths and faces; and lastly their bodies were hacked into four quarters, to be nailed up over the front door of their dwelling-houses, whilst their heads impaled were fixed in some conspicuous place.

It is with relief we turn to the scanty details of the burial of these poor victims of Tudor brutality. Their remains were gathered together by the Hospitallers of St. John of Jerusalem at Clerkenwell[2] and placed in their Friary cart kept for the purpose, which was covered with black, with a large white Cross along the length of it, and a small St. John's Cross in front; whilst a bell attached rang out notifying to the people of its approach. It was one of the seven corporal works of mercy carried out by the Knights of St. John to fetch the remains of felons executed at Tyburn, and bury them in Pardon Churchyard, a place of burial between their Hospital at Clerkenwell, and the London Charterhouse; where in a chapel on the site prayer might be offered on behalf of their souls. In the present instance the two friars and the nun were not interred at Pardon Churchyard, but were taken to the Grey Friars House[3] in Newgate Street close

---

[1] *Henry VIII and the English Monasteries*, I, 150, referring to Bourchier's *Hist. Eccl. de Martyrio F.F. Ord. Min.* 1582.

[2] As a Knight of Grace of the Order of St. John I cannot but express gratification that after 400 years the Order is still engaged in works of mercy both during war and in time of peace.—C. C.

[3] *Chron. Grey Fr.*, Camden Society, p. 37.

by, where they were buried in the churchyard of one of the most beautiful churches in London.

There is one other matter in connexion with the above tragedy, which, though it has nothing whatever to do with the Friars Minor, is of interest to us in Canterbury. It will be remembered that Elizabeth Barton was professed at St. Sepulchre's Nunnery. In due course this House was suppressed and the nuns turned adrift, its lands, revenues, and ornaments appropriated by the King, and the place given over to secular uses. The last Prioress, Dame Philippa John, evidently had no love for King Henry, who had murdered her friends, and despoiled her of her home and goods; when therefore she came to make her will [1] in 1542 she, in the enumeration of his Royal Titles places him as "*Supreme Head in* ~~Hell~~ (so crossed out) *earth, next under GOD, of the Church of England and Ireland.*" This was certainly rank treason, but she knew that by the time her will would be made public, she herself would be safe from this Tudor tyrant.

[1] Canterbury Wills Archdeaconry, Vol. XXVI, § 1.

CHAPTER VI.

THE DISSOLUTION.

HASTED in his *History of Kent* says that the Canterbury House was dissolved in 1534, but this is evidently incorrect. In April, 1534, a commission was issued to George Browne, Prior of the Augustinian Hermits, whom the King appointed Provincial of the Order, and John Hilsey, Provincial of the Friars Preachers, to visit the houses of all friars to enquire concerning their life and morals, and to instruct them how to conduct themselves. It was also proposed that they should be assembled in their Chapter-houses and examined separately concerning their faith and obedience to Henry VIII, and bound by an oath of allegiance to him, Queen Anne and their issue.[1]

The Conventuals seem generally to have accepted the oath : the Observants offered resistance. At Canterbury only two friars—Mychelsen and John Game—are expressly mentioned as having refused the oath.[2] But two others—Judocus of Amsterdam and Lewis Wilkinson—died there, and another, Christopher Burrell, went mad.[3] Some brethren were sent away for safe custody and others fled abroad.[4]

The history of the four years 1534-8 is obscure. A few days before 17 June, 1534, two cartloads of friars were seen being driven through London to the Tower.[5] But at this time (1 and 13 June) the Warden of Canterbury, Friar Bernardine Covert,[6]

---

[1] *L. and P. Hen. VIII*, VII, 587 (18), 590 ; *Arch. Cant.*, XXXIV, 87.
[2] *Ibid.* VII, App. 27.   [3] *Ibid.* VII, 1607.
[4] Thus a Dutch Observant, who was employed " to blot the bishop of Rome's name out of the books " fled abroad with a companion, after being called a heretic and spat upon by Henry Bocher, another Observant : *L. and P. Hen. VIII*, IX, 789.
[5] *Ibid.* VII, 856.
[6] Friars Bernardine Covert and Thomas Roche, Observants, were authorized by Henry VIII, on 24 January, 1534, to go to Calais to " declare the gospel and the word of God." P.R.O., E. 135, Bdl. 2, no. 13.

wrote to Lady Lisle at Calais that he " had made a quiet end with my Lord of Canterbury " : [1] this appears to mean that some arrangement was being made for the continuance of the convent. But on 11 August, Chapuys the Ambassador wrote to the Emperor Charles V that " of the seven [2] houses of Observants five have been already emptied of friars because they have refused to swear to the Statutes made against the Pope. Those in the two others expect also to be expelled." And on 29 August he wrote : " All the Observants have been driven out of their monasteries for refusing the oath against the Holy See." [3]

Yet Observant Friars certainly continued to live at Canterbury, under the rule of a Conventual warden. Before the month of March in 1535, the King, " against the heart of the Provincial," had appointed Friar John Arture or Arthur as Warden ; he was a man of bad reputation, [4] and treated the members with great severity, " because they rebelled against the King and held so stiffly to the Bishop of Rome, for which he daily reproved them." Eventually Friar John Arthur got into trouble for blaming " these new books and new preachers," and defending pilgrimages in a sermon preached on Passion Sunday, 1535, at the Parish Church at Herne. [5] He was informed against by Friar Henry Bocher, an Observant whom he had imprisoned ; the result was that the latter was set free, and Friar John Arthur was himself imprisoned ; he, however, fearing worse trouble escaped, and fled overseas to France.

The Provincial Minister hereupon appointed Arthur's " mortal enemy " to be Warden ; he favoured the Observants, but, according to Arthur, was so ignorant that he could not construe his paternoster. [6] Who this was does not appear. Citizens of Canterbury still continued to make bequests to the Grey Friars and to desire burial in their cemetery ; and in a will dated 11 January, 1537, they are still called the Observant Friars. [7]

---

[1] *L. and P. Hen. VIII*, VII, 765, 837. Lord Lisle at this time authorized the collection of money to help the Canterbury Friars, see p. 50 above. Another supporter of the Canterbury Observants was John Hales, of the Dungeon, baron of the Exchequer : cf. *L. and P. Hen. VIII*, IX, 789.
[2] The seventh house may have been that in Guernsey.
[3] *L. and P. Hen. VIII*, IX, 1057, 1095.　　[4] *Grey Fr. Oxf.*, Little, p. 285.
[5] *L. and P. Hen. VIII*, VIII, 480 ; IX, 789.
[6] *Ibid*. VII, 765 ; VIII, 480.　　[7] See Appendix III.

On 5 May, 1538, the King gave a commission to Richard Ingworth, the newly appointed Bishop of Dover to visit the English Friaries and take possession of their seals and their keys, sequestrate their goods, and make inventories of the same. Ingworth did not reach Canterbury till 13 December, and the only note we have of the suppression of this House is the letter written by him to Thomas Cromwell, possibly on the 15th, the day after the friars were turned out ; he writes :—

My syngular goode lorde, In my humble manner, pleseyth youe to understonde that I have receyueyd the howse of Whyte fryers in Aylyforde in to the Kyngs hands, and the XIII day of December I cam to Canterbury wher yt I fynde iii howseys, more in dètt than all yt they have ys abull to pay, and specyally ye Austen fryers . . . the black and grey be abull wᵗ. ther implements to pay ther detts and for owr costs, and lytyll more . . . and so this Sonday I woll make an ende in Canterbury, and on Munday to Sandwyche.[1]

Local records and tradition alike are silent with regard to the details of these doings. In this case even the Public Record Office does not contain either the Deed of Suppression or the Letter of Submission with which it was accompanied. As however, these were " common form " as far as the Franciscan Friaries were concerned (they were used with merely blanks in the wording for the dates to be inserted and to suit the different localities), and were certainly used in the suppression of the Grey Friars at Stamford, Coventry, Bedford, Aylesbury, and London,[2] it is certain that similar documents were offered to the members of the Canterbury House for their signature, and as a last corporate act for the application of their Convent Seal. The Letter of Submission is such a curious document that it seems worth printing here : its author was probably Cromwell and one can scarcely envy Richard Ingworth, the Bishop of Dover, himself a Black Friar, in the execution of this business. The letter is as follows, the actual date is of course conjectural :—

For as moche as we, the Warden and Freers of the howse of Saynt Francis in [Cantorburye] commonly called the Gray Freers in [Cantorburye] doo profoundly consider that the perficcion of Christian liuyng doth not conciste in dome ceremonies, weryng of a grey cootte, disgeasing our selfe

[1] P.R.O. Misc. Letters *temp.* Henry VIII, ser. 2, Vol. VIII, p. 114 ; *L. and P. Hen. VIII*, XIII, pt. II, 1058.
[2] *Deputy Keeper's 8th Report*, Appendix II : Kingsford, *Grey Fr. of London*, 217.

5

aftyr straunge fassions, dokynge, nodyngs and bekynge, in gurdyng our selffs wythe a gurdle full of knots, and other like Papisticall ceremonyes, wherein we have byn moost pryncipally practysed and misselyd in tymes past, but the very tru waye to please God, and to liue a tru Christian man, wyth oute all ypocrasie and fayned dissimalacion, is sincerely declaryd vnto vs by owre Master Christe, his Euangelists and Apostles : Being mindyd hereafter to follow the same, conformyng oure selffe vnto the will and pleasure of our supreme hed vndre God in erthe, the Kings Majestie ; and not to follow hensforth the supersticious tradicions of ony foryncicall potentate or peere, wythe mutuall assent and consent doo submytt owrselffes vnto the mercy of our saide Soveraygn Lorde. And wythe like mutuall assent and consent doo surrender and yelde vpe into the hands of the same, all owr saide howse of Saynt Francis comenly callyd the Gray Freers in [Cantorburye] wythe all lands, tenements, gardens, meadows, waters, pondyards, fedyngs, pastures, comens, rentes reuersions and all other owr interest, ryghtes or titles aperteynyng vnto the same, mooste humbly besechyng his moost noble grace to disspose of vs and of the same, as best schall stonde wythe his mooste graciouse pleasure, and further frely to grant vnto euery on of vs his licens vndre wretyng and seall, to chaunge owr habites into secular fassion, and to receve suche maner of livyngs as other secular Priestes comenly be preferryd vnto. And we alle faythfully schall pray vnto Allmyghty God to preserue his mooste noble Grace, wythe increse of moche felicitie and honor. And in witnes of alle and singular the premysses, we the said Warden and Convent of the Gray Freers in [Cantorburye] to thes presentes haue putte owr Couent Seale the [xiiii day of Decembre] in the thirtyth yere of the raygn of owr mooste souerayne Kinge Henry the yeght, or Anno 1538.

The Deed of Surrender was in Latin, a purely formal and legal instrument and a "common form" with blanks to suit the descriptions of the persons surrendering and the places surrendered. The Deed executed by the members of the Canterbury House has not been found, but was doubtless signed and sealed by the Brethren on the eventful day, as Henry was always a stickler for legal procedure in everything he did. Nor has any Inventory of the friars' movables been found or any "pension list"; they doubtless each received the sum of five shillings and were allowed to depart where they would.

One is arrested at this juncture to compare the characters of the two persons—curiously both named Richard Ingworth—who had to do with the beginning of the Franciscan movement in this country, and the end of it.

The first Richard Ingworth, according to Eccleston, formed one of the band of nine Franciscans who came to England in 1224, already mentioned, with Agnellus at their head. He was an elderly priest, and according to the same authority, was the first Franciscan Friar who preached to the people north of the Alps. He went from Canterbury to London and then to Oxford, where he founded the celebrated Friary whose members became of European reputation on account of their learning. He also founded the Northampton House ; and afterwards became the *Custos* of the Cambridge Custody. He held the position of Vicar of the English Province, whilst Agnellus was abroad, and afterwards became first Provincial of Ireland, and lastly he went as a missionary to the Holy Land, where he died.[1] Dr. Jessopp in *The Coming of the Friars* sums him up as "a man who had made his mark and was famous as a preacher, of rare gifts and deep earnestness."

The later Richard Ingworth[2] was a Black Friar, a member of the Friary of King's Langley, the same Order to which Dr. John Hilsey belonged, who afterwards as Provincial of it received the commission from Henry in 1534 to visit the Friaries and reduce them to obedience. Ingworth had taken the degree of B.D. in 1525, the same year as Hilsey; and had in 1526 been authorized by the Master-General to proceed to that of D.D. in any university, subject to the assent of his Province.[3] In due course Ingworth became Prior of King's Langley and he held that office at the time the Priory was visited by Hilsey on 5 May, 1534, for the purpose of extracting from its members the Oath of Supremacy which Ingworth signed for the whole establish-

---

[1] *Eccleston*, ed. Little, 4-14, 44. *Franciscan Province of Ireland* (B.S.F.S.), XI-XVII.

[2] Canon Scott Robertson's *Richard Ingworth, the first Bishop of Dover.*

[3] So far the university from which Ingworth obtained his degrees is not known, but as he received licence from the Master-General of the Dominican Order to do so, he probably did proceed in some university. From the Registers at Rome of the Master-General the following is extracted :—

Registrum primum Vicarii Ordinis, Mag'ri Francisci Silvestri instituti xxxi Julii, 1524, qui in Mag'rm Gen. electus est Junii 3, 1525, fol. 107.

Annus 1525.

Reverendo Patri Magiro Roberto de Milis provinciali [Anglie] conceditur seu intimatur, quatenus habentur approbati infrascripti, ut possint promoveri ad gradum magisterii . . . ad baccalariam vero Ricardus Ynguurthe . . . et licenciantur, ut ad dictos gradus possint promoveri in aliquâ Universitate, et accipere dictos gradus, premisso prius examine rigoroso per viros doctos, et de assensu provincie. [Dat.] v Julii, Romae.

1526, Anno ij.

Fratri Ricardo Ingwurth, baccharlaris, conceditur, quod possit promoveri ad Magisterium in aliquâ Universitate, de assensu tamen Provinciae . . . iiij . . . Augusti, Romae.

Op. cit.

ment : " Ego Ricardus Ingerth, Prior Conventus predicatorum Langley Regis, cum assensu omnium fratrum conventus predicti, non coactus sed sponte, subscribo." [1]

Such easy compliance and possibly an old friendship resulted in Ingworth joining Hilsey on his visitation tours, where for the business in hand he was active, discreet, and apt. Hilsey was rewarded by his promotion to the Bishopric of Rochester, and Ingworth on 19 December, 1537, was consecrated in a small Chapel at the west end of old St. Paul's, as Bishop of Dover, being the first to hold that Suffragan See. Three weeks afterwards he [2] received two royal commissions to "visit and vex" his brother friars ; the first, power to depose suspected superiors and to appoint others in their stead ; and the second to visit all the Friaries, "take possession of their seals, keys, sequestrate their goods, and to make inventories of the same." Ingworth was still Prior of King's Langley till it was suppressed in 1538-9, and then was rewarded by the grant of it to himself. He also was given the Rectory of Chiddingstone, Kent, in 1539—and held much other property (in the same county) which belonged to the King's Langley House, and had formerly been part of the possessions of the great heiress Juliana de Leybourne.

With all his activities in assisting Cromwell in driving the friars from their Houses, and at times to a cruel death (for was he not responsible for the execution of Friar Stone [3] of the Canterbury House of Austin Friars, on the Dane John, Canterbury, in 1538 ?); he sometimes failed to go the length Cromwell required. On one occasion being reprimanded for not desecrating the Friary Church at Droitwich, and alarmed by the taunt that "though he had changed his friar's habit he had not changed his friar's heart," he writes :—" God shall be my judge, my friar's heart was gone two years before my habit, saving only my living." [4]

It is with relief that we turn to the last phase in the mediæval history of this House, which will not detain us long. We

---

[1] Close, 26 Hen. VIII, m. 15. (14) d.
[2] *Hen. VIII, and Eng. Mon.*, Gasquet (1889), Vol. II, p. 244.
[3] Ellis, *Orig. L., 3rd Series iij.* 181 ; *Hist. MSS. Comm. 9th Report, Appendix*, p. 153 ; and also A. Cope, *Dialogi Sex*, p. 373.
[4] *Supp. Monast.*, 197.

hear no more of the Canterbury Friars,[1] and nothing of the Friary until the small quarrels and wrangling begin over the spoil.

As early as 5 October, 1538[2] (i.e. before the House had been actually dissolved), Archbishop Cranmer wrote to Cromwell that "as the Grey Friars, Canterbury, is very commodious for my servant Thomas Cobham, brother to Lord Cobham, I beg you will help him to the said house." But Thomas Cobham was to be disappointed,[3] as in February 1539, the place was let to Thomas Spylman, the local receiver of the Court of Augmentations, for 40s. a year. Then on 3 March occurs the following letter from Sir Christopher Hales to Cromwell :—[4]

"My fellow Spylman who is here, one of the receivers of the Augmentations, has before this enterprized to meddle with the house lately belonging to the Grey Friars of Canterbury, and, as he says, by your Worship's direction. He now tells me that Batherst, whom I have heard, the King wishes to dwell in Canterbury for the erection of cloth-making, has lately informed him that the King intends him to have the said house, and he has asked him for the keys of it, which Spylman has refused. If Batherst or another of the best clothiers in Kent were disposed to set up cloth making in Canterbury, the house of Black Friars would be sufficient for the purpose, but I hear he insists on having the Grey Friars. Canterbury, 3 March."

Spylman, supported by Cromwell, won the day ; and in the following July he bought the whole site including the Church and Bell Tower for £100,[5] Batherst having to be content with a lease of a part of the Blackfriars. In 1544[6] Spylman sold the premises to Thomas Rolf for £200. The property consisted of two messuages, two orchards, two gardens, three acres of [arable] land, ten acres of meadow, and four acres of pasture with pertinencies in the Parishes of St. Peter, St. Mildred, and St. Margaret, all held in chief of the Crown.[7] It was this Rolf who, in 1549,

---

[1] An ex-Minorite who played a part in Canterbury and elsewhere as chaplain to Archbishop Cranmer and a zealous reformer was John Joseph, D.D. ; but there is no evidence that he had been a member of the Canterbury House as suggested by Mr. Little, *Grey Fr. in Oxf.*, p. 288.

[2] *L. and P. Hen. VIII*, XIII, ii, 537.   [3] *Ibid.* XIV, i. 609.

[4] 3 March, 1539. *Ibid.*, XIV (pt. i.), 423.

[5] *Ibid.* XIV, i. 423. According to Weever, *Fun. Mon.* 238, the house was valued at the suppression at £39 12s. 8½d. of yearly revenue. There is certainly some confusion here, but the origin of the error has not been traced.

[6] Hasted's *Kent*, IV, 447-8.

[7] P.R.O. Feet of Fines, Henry VIII, Bdle. 53, File 383, no. 18 : printed in *Archæol. Cant.* XXXIV, 91. Hasted, IV, 448, gives five acres of meadow.

obtained leave of the City to stop up the carriage way from St. Peter's Street to the Friary, by reducing it to the narrow passage which still exists. In the Collection by Alderman Bunce, already referred to, are copies of the Letters Patent conveying to Thomas Spylman and Isabella his wife, the House and site of the Grey Friars, dated at Tyrling 17 July, 31 Henry VIII (1539), and of the Fine levied and other documents conveying the property from Thomas Spylman and Isabella, his wife, to Thomas Rolf, dated 20 January and 2 February, 1544.

From the inquisition[1] post-mortem of William Lovelace, taken 29 September, 1578, it appears that Thomas Rolf granted the property to Lovelace and others on 16 February, 1565-6, and that it was assigned by them to Thomas Rolf's widow for her life, in compensation for her dower, 10 November, 1567; and that she afterwards married one Erasmus Finch. William Lovelace,[2] Sergeant-at-Law, who died in 1577, was seized of this property; by his Will dated July 1576, he left to his son and heir, William Lovelace, *inter alia*, "one house and site of the Grey Friars in the City of Canterbury." The latter was baptized in 1561, and was married to Elizabeth Aucher of Bishopsbourne; he lived at the Grey Friars, and was afterwards knighted. In 1589 he covenanted with the Mayor and Commonalty to take down the stone bridge which led from Lamb Lane to the Friary, but apparently left one arch remaining. He died in 1629, and was the last of his family to live in Canterbury. His son, also Sir William Lovelace, kt., was of Woolwich, and it was the latter's fourth son, Richard, who was the celebrated Colonel and Cavalier Poet, also of Woolwich.

Afterwards the Friary came into possession of the Hartcup family, of whom Thomas Hartcup was here in 1799.

The property remained in the Hartcup family during the early part of the nineteenth century, and later it appears to have passed into the possession of a Miss Mary C. Gravatt, a cousin of

[1] See footnote to a note on " The Grey Friars of Canterbury," by Miss Churchill, in *Arch. Cant.* Vol. XXXIV, p. 91.
[2] He was of the old Kentish family of Lovelace of Lovelace Place, Bethersden, whose ancestor John L. purchased that property in 1367. William L. was of Gray's Inn 1548, called to the Bar 1551, elected M.P., Canterbury 1558, Sergeant-at-Law 1567, and died 23 March 1577, and was buried in the Cathedral. For the history of this family, see *Arch. Cant.* X, p. 184.

that family. She died in 1865, leaving by will the property to her brother, William Gravatt, Esq., who also by will left it to certain devisees who conveyed different parts of the property to various people as garden ground, etc. Ultimately in 1898 it came into the possession of a Mr. D. H. Hodgkinson, who died 25 October, 1916, whose nephew, Mr. W. Hodgkinson, conveyed the building known as the Grey Friars, the site of the church, the churchyard and other ground surrounding the site, to Major H. G. James in 1919.

Major James has thoroughly restored the building in a truly conservative manner, and has laid out the gardens with artistic grace, so that this ancient Religious House has now a beautiful setting as well as a romantic and tragic past.

CHAPTER VII.

THE RESTORATION OF THE REMAINING DOMESTIC BUILDING.

BY ROBERT H. GOODSALL, A.R.I.B.A., A.I.STRUCT.E., ARCHITECT.

IN June, 1919, the owner of the site of the Franciscan monastery at Canterbury, Major H. G. James, decided to undertake the restoration of the only portion of the buildings remaining above the ground, i.e. the structure which spans the small arm of the Stour standing to the south-east of the church.

The building structurally was in a moderately sound state of preservation, but during the centuries following upon the dissolution it had obviously been adapted to many uses which had very materially altered its original character.

It was the wish of Major James that these secular alterations should be removed and the building restored to its original form, at the same time carrying out all necessary structural repairs as far as possible in character with the old work.

A survey which I made of the building disclosed the following facts :—

The transverse walls were built upon solid foundations of "tufa" on either bank of the river, the same stone occurring in the retaining walls of the banks both above and below the building. The cross walls were carried upon pointed arches springing from the wall abutment on either side, and two circular columns and capitals rising from the bed of the stream.

The nature of the bases of these shafts, if any exist, it was impossible to determine, the river bottom having risen considerably during the course of centuries. It was impracticable at the time to dam the stream, an operation which might easily be carried out, and so settle an interesting point.

66

The capitals of these two shafts were badly weather worn, and the mouldings were somewhat difficult to analyse. It is possible that the stones formed bases of Norman shafts prior to being built into their present position.

Above the ground level on either bank the walling was of flint and random stone, with wrought stone dressings, and with repairs and additions carried out in narrow brickwork. Generally this walling was in a good state of preservation, requiring little more than pointing here and there, and a few of the quoin stones and other dressings renewing.

Much of the tiling of the roof was in a defective state due to decay in the rafters and tiling battens beneath.

Two large windows on the south-east elevation, two dormer windows, and one or more chimney stacks were obviously late additions to the original building.

The building was entered by a doorway placed centrally in the north-west elevation, giving access to a narrow passage and staircase, the latter of no great age. The level of the entrance floor was approximately the same as the ground.

A wooden screen, probably eighteenth century work, divided the passage from the large room to the eastward, the boards of this partition bearing a number of carvings of names and dates, the work of different occupants of the place.

The smaller room to the westward was divided from the passage and staircase by ancient timber framing of original work, lighted by two small windows looking on to the river, also original.

This room had been used in comparatively modern times as a " lock-up "; and latterly as a kitchen; in one corner was a modern copper and flue.

An awkward flight of stairs with winders led to two corresponding rooms on the first floor, divided from the passage and staircase by similar partitions as on the ground floor.

The passage was lit by a small window at the south-west end, probably a late seventeenth century addition, and a small tortuous staircase of winders led to the two attics on the top floor.

The floor of the smaller of the two rooms on the first floor was at a considerably lower level than the larger room, two steps leading down into it. The room was lit by a narrow lancet window, which above the springing of the arch had been filled in solid, to form a fireplace for the attic above. At one side of the window was a large fireplace, the opening of which had been considerably reduced in size by rubble infilling to accommodate a modern grate.

The larger of the two rooms on the first floor corresponded to the room below, but had the dividing screen between it and the passage at a different angle. A fireplace stood on the north-west wall towards the north corner, and the room was lit by three windows, a lancet in the gable end, a narrow square headed window, with an internal splay on one reveal only in the eastern corner, and a large casement window of much later character.

In the roof were two attics, each lit by a small dormer window—not original work. As mentioned above, the south-west attic had a fireplace built into the head of the lancet window of the gable.

The whole of the roof timbers were hidden by laths and plaster in a more or less dilapidated state but suggesting a fine roof underneath.

This much it was possible to ascertain by preliminary inspection, and the next step was to clear away all plaster which was obscuring old work on walls, roof, and ceilings.

The plastering of the roof in the attics was first removed and some fine timbers in excellent state of preservation were exposed.

By referring to the accompanying scale drawings of the elevations it will be noticed that the pitch of the roof is not the same throughout its length, the smaller or south-west portion being steeper and springing from a lower wall plate. The ridge, except for irregularities due to age, was level throughout its length. The break in the roof occurred above the timber framed partition which divides the two portions of the building.

An inspection of the inside of the roof revealed the fact that the timbers in the south-west end were more decayed and had the appearance of greater age than those in the other part of the roof. There is, I think, little doubt that this is part of the original roof, and of the same date as the main walling.

68

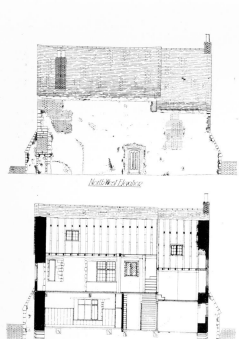

North-West Elevation

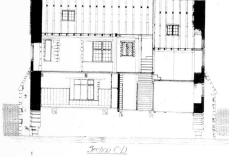

Section C-D

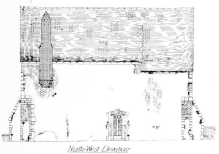

North-West Elevation

South-West Elevation

The Grey Friars, Canterbury
Before Restoration

South-West Elevation

The Grey Friars, Canterbury
After Restoration

Section C-D

Scale $\frac{1}{20}$th inch = 1 foot.

GREY FRIARS, CANTERBURY.—NORTH-WEST AND SOUTH-WEST ELEVATIONS
Robert H. Goodsall, A.R.I.B.A., A.I.Struct.E., Tankerton-on-Sea

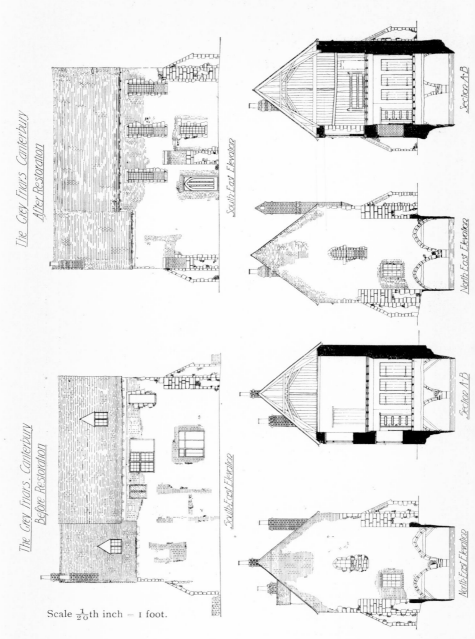

The Grey Friars Canterbury
After Restoration

South-East Elevation

Section A-B

North-East Elevation

The Grey Friars, Canterbury
Before Restoration

Scale $\frac{1}{20}$th inch = 1 foot.

South-East Elevation

North-East Elevation

Section A-B

GREY FRIARS, CANTERBURY—SOUTH-EAST AND NORTH-EAST ELEVATIONS

Robert H. Goodsall, A.R.I.B.A., A.I.Struct.E., Tankerton-on-Sea

The roof over the north-east part of the building was constructed of timbers of larger section and appeared to have been used in some earlier building, subsequently adapted to their present use. Many of the rafters and collars had mortice holes which obviously had not been cut for the present construction, and must have been wrought when the timbers formed part of some other roof; it is not impossible that they were taken from the Friars' Church upon its demolition.

Reference to the drawings of the elevations will show that below the wall plate of this part of the roof, and in the walling of the north-east gable end is a band of brickwork some 2 feet high, and comparison with the older part of the roof will show that this corresponds to the additional amount of walling required to allow for the difference in pitch between the two.

From these facts I think it is safe to assume that at some time the original roof over this part of the building became defective and was replaced by the timbers from another roof which were for some reason available, and the walling was raised by adding courses of brickwork as we see it, to permit of an alteration in pitch. If this supposition is correct it goes far to prove that the south-west portion of the roof is the older and probably original work.

A number of the roof rafters were defective, some through decay and others because a part had been cut away when the dormer windows were inserted, and for the construction of fireplaces, etc., and it was found necessary to strip the roof and entirely reconstruct it, replacing a certain amount of timber by new oak.

The next part of the building to be dealt with was the flooring of the attics, which evidently never formed part of the original structure, and must have been a comparatively late addition. Upon removing the boards, the spaces between the joists were found to be filled with sand, the whole weight of which was carried by the laths and plaster, in fact sand was found below all floors except the entrance floor. A careful search revealed a number of small articles of varying age and of considerable interest hidden in the sand. No doubt the sand was used in this position as a sound deadener.

The construction of the attic floor was of the most haphazard character; in fact the joists of the larger floor were carried upon the central tie beam which in one place had been cut through to as much as two-thirds of its depth to allow of a door-way being constructed, and at one end took its bearing upon a shallow plate above the wide casement window. Considering the weight of the floor with the additional weight of the sand packed between the joists it is a wonder that this plate did not give way.

The whole of the attic flooring which in parts was much decayed was taken down, together with the very awkward staircase of winders which led to it, and a better idea of the original apartments could then be gained.

At the same time the fireplace which filled the head of the lancet in the south-west gable was swept away, together with its flue, and the window restored to its original proportions.

The curtain arch of this window closing in the splayed reveals on the inside had apparently been originally constructed with thick tiles or narrow bricks, for a fragment of old tiling was found beneath the plaster at the springing. The new arch, necessitated by the removal of the chimney breast and flue was accordingly rebuilt in this manner.

The corresponding window at the opposite end of the building was apparently never arched over above the splayed reveals; at any rate careful investigation failed to produce any evidence to this effect; and the oak lintel which spanned the opening was left in position.

The removal of the attic flooring and staircase had the effect of producing two fine rooms, divided by the original timber framed partition, with a magnificent timber roof.

Before the winter set in the problem of reconstructing this roof was tackled. As already mentioned some of the rafters had been cut through when the dormer windows were built in, and others to allow flues to pass through, while still more were badly decayed at their feet. Much of the lathing upon which the tiles were hung was defective, and the only practical method of restoration was to dismantle the roof section by section, and rebuild. This was the method adopted. All the old material

70

which was sound was re-used including the tiling. The result was a strong and sound roof which should last for many years. Much of the beautiful colouring and texture of the old tiling was inevitably lost with the re-arrangement of the tiles, but the kindly influence of the weather during a few years will do much to obliterate the effect of apparent newness. Subsequently the spaces between the rafters on the inside were plastered.

Before and during the reconstruction of the roof much work was done by the masons to the walling of the structure.

Study of the south-east elevation revealed several interesting pieces of evidence of alteration. The single light window at the east corner was found to have been entirely changed from its original proportion, or rather in its position in relation to the height of the building.

When the roof was raised the head of the window was raised a corresponding amount, so that the new relative position of head and eaves was the same as the old. At the same time the sill of the window was raised a similar amount.

The realization of this led to the discovery that the floor of this room had likewise been raised, probably when the alteration was made to the roof. At its present height, floor and window sill are practically level. No doubt the original level of the floor was the same as in the smaller room at the north-west end, of which the old original boarding was discovered beneath later flooring. The height of the window sills above the original floor level would have been about 2 feet.

Evidence internally beneath the plaster, and externally on the walling led to the discovery that there had been three such windows along the length of the room, the two north-westerly ones having been partially destroyed when the large casement window, and the small one which lit the staircase were inserted. This point was conclusively proved by the finding of the reveal stones both externally and upon the internal splay.

In all three windows the internal reveals were splayed upon the north-west side only. This curious arrangement is difficult to account for, unless it was for the purpose of allowing more light to enter in the early morning.

The two casement windows were both removed and the two

71

original single light windows reformed, their proportions being kept the same as the easterly one.

As the sills of these windows and also the window in the gable were level with the floor, a small screen wall supporting a false sill was built up in each case.

The fireplace in this room which was not original was removed but the flue was retained, in case some form of heating should be required at any time, and a simple chimney stack in brickwork was designed to harmonize with the roof lines.

In the small south-west room the original fireplace was opened up. There is, I think, little doubt that this fireplace is contemporary with the main structure; the curious way in which the jamb breaks into the reveal of the lancet certainly suggests this; it is an interesting example of an early fireplace, and beyond necessary structural repairs was left untouched.

It was decided not to lower the first floor to its original level, particularly as the entrance floor had also been raised. In the river walls the stone templates which carried the beams of the floor may be seen, fixing conclusively the original level. Probably the gradual silting up of the river would account for the raising of the ground floor and floors above.

The large casement window in the north-east room of the ground floor can hardly have been original, but no traces of any earlier window could be found. The small window in the gable end would not adequately light the room alone and consequently the present single light window was constructed lineable with the window above, and the remainder of the walling filled in. The justification of this must be utility and is not based on evidence; in this light it must be judged.

In the small south-west room which had been used as a kitchen the copper was removed, and the two small windows were put in a sound state, the defective masonry being replaced.

An important point which next had to be settled was the question of the staircase. It was obvious that the existing makeshift affair was a crude addition, and there was no evidence to show where the original one had been, or if one existed at all.

Personally I am of the opinion that the halls on the upper, i.e. first floor, were entered at their own level from an outside staircase, and also from the adjacent domestic buildings which have disappeared but of which the foundations can be traced.

There is evidence of buildings abutting the building on both sides of the river ; these are indicated in old prints.

The ground floor rooms were no doubt approached by one or more doors on one or both sides of the river.

Under the circumstances the question of following an original model did not arise, and the present staircase was designed in as simple a character as possible to meet existing requirements.

The original screen wall of timber framing which divided the building was overhauled and put into a sound state, and the doorway on the south-east elevation was re-opened.

Externally the existence of several additional buttresses was proved, and these were rebuilt, the character of the old ones being copied. The stonework, flintwork, and brickwork generally was overhauled and put into a sound state.

Throughout the work the aim was to retain as much of the old materials and character of the building as possible, consistent with the task in hand. The contractor was Mr. Walter Cozens of Canterbury, and the work was carried on under the personal superintendence of his representative Mr. W. E. Taylor, to whose appreciation and love of antiquity the success of the restoration is in a great measure due. In cases where the work was of a particularly difficult nature Mr. Taylor carried out the task with his own hands, and at all times his knowledge of Gothic tradition and his able suggestions were of the utmost value.

British Society of Franciscan Studies.

The following are works already issued by the Society :—

Vol. I.   Liber Exemplorum ad usum prædicantium, edited by A. G. Little, 1908.

Vol. II.   Fratris Johannis Pecham Tractatus Tres De Paupertate, edited by C. L. Kingsford, A. G. Little, and F. Tocco, 1910.

Vol. III.   Fratris Rogeri Bacon Compendium Studii Theologiæ, edited by H. Rashdall, 1911.

Extra Series, I.   Franciscan Essays, by Paul Sabatier and others, 1912.

Vol. IV.   Opus Tertium (part of) of Roger Bacon, edited by A. G. Little, 1912.

Vol. V.   Collectanea Franciscana I, edited by A. G. Little, M. R. James, and H. M. Bannister, 1914.

Vol. VI.   Grey Friars of London, edited by C. L. Kingsford, 1915.

Vol. VII.   Blessed Agnes of Bohemia, edited by W. W. Seton, 1915.

Vol. VIII.   Blessed Giles of Assisi, edited by W. W. Seton, 1918.

Vol. IX.   Franciscan Province of Ireland, edited by Rev. E. B. Fitzmaurice, O.F.M., and A. G. Little, 1920.

Vol. X.   Collectanea Franciscana II, edited by C. L. Kingsford 1922.

Vol. XI.   Nicholas Glassberger and His Works, edited by W. W. Seton, 1923.

Extra Series II The Grey Friars of Canterbury by C. Cotton, 1924.

Forthcoming Works.

Speculum Perfectionis, edited by Paul Sabatier.

Medical Treatises of Roger Bacon, edited by A. G. Little and E. Withington.

SUBSCRIPTIONS.—Minimum Subscription : Members, 10/6 ; Associates, 2/6.   It is requested that subscriptions should be sent at the beginning of the year to the Hon. Treasurer, Dr. Walter Seton, University College, London, Gower Street, London, W.C.1., to whom all enquiries should be addressed.